D0462478

GREEN
CLEAN

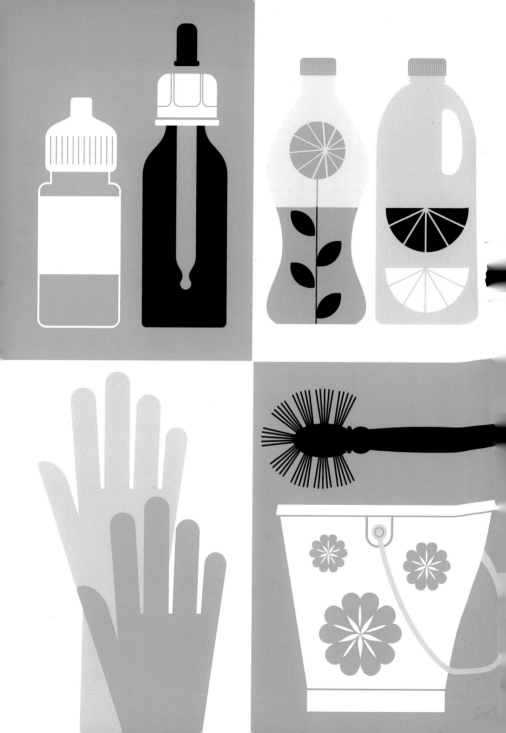

GREEN
CLEAN

The Environmentally Sound Guide to Cleaning Your Home

By Linda Mason Hunter & Mikki Halpin

MELCHER
MEDIA

DuraBooks are completely waterproof.
For best results, dry in an open, ventilated
area, or hand dry with a towel.

Acknowledgments

Linda Mason Hunter: Thanks to Kelly Roberson, my research assistant, who keeps me on target and on time; and to my two grandmothers, Nelle and Hasel.

Mikki Halpin: Thanks to my neighbors, who've read the countless inspirational and informational notes on various green topics that I've left in the lobby over the years. Here it is in one book!

Melcher Media thanks Lina Burton, Janine James, David McAninch, Janie Matthews, Lauren Nathan, Lia Ronnen, Holly Rothman, Kevin Szell, Alex Tart, Shoshana Thaler, Paula White, and Megan Worman.

Published by

MELCHER MEDIA

124 West 13th Street
New York, NY 10011
www.melcher.com

Publisher: Charles Melcher
Editor in Chief: Duncan Bock
Editor: David E. Brown
Production Director: Andrea Hirsh
Publishing Manager: Bonnie Eldon
Editorial Assistant: Lindsey Stanberry

Distributed in the US by
DK Publishing
www.dk.com

© 2005 Melcher Media, Inc.
Chapters 1, 7, and 8 © 2005 Linda Mason Hunter
Illustrations on pages 2, 6, 26, 44, 68, 80, 100, 112, 130, 146, 158, and 174 © 2005 Sean Sims

DuraBook™, patent no. 6,773,034, is a trademark of Melcher Media, Inc. The DuraBook™ format utilizes revolutionary technology and is completely waterproof and highly durable.

All trademarks are property of their respective owners.
The information in this book has been carefully researched, and all efforts have been made to ensure accuracy. Neither the publisher nor the writers can assume any responsibility for any accident, injuries, losses, or other damages resulting from the use of this book.

All rights reserved. No part of this publication may be reproduced, stored in a retrieval system, or transmitted in any form or by any means, electronic, mechanical, photocopying, recording, or otherwise, without prior consent of the publishers.

08   10 9 8 7 6

Design by The Moderns
Cover Photo by Dylan Cross Photography, NYC

Printed in China

ISBN 10: 1-59591-004-2
ISBN 13: 978-1-59591-004-2

Library of Congress Control Number: 2005000866

CONTENTS

1 : GOING GREEN

IT ALL STARTED WITH A BOX OF BAKING
SODA. I HAD NEVER THOUGHT TO USE IT
BEYOND WHIPPING UP A BATCH OF COOK-
IES UNTIL MY GRANDMOTHER PLACED A
NEWLY OPENED BOX IN THE BACK OF MY
REFRIGERATOR, TELLING ME WITH A WINK
THAT IT GOT RID OF ODORS.

Baking soda is a little bit of household magic: an odor neutralizer, cleanser, and air freshener all in one. For common everyday grime, it soon replaced my commercial abrasive for cleaning sinks and countertops.

Before long, out went the glass cleaner. Even with its antiseptic smell and unnatural blue color, it didn't make my windows sparkle any better than club soda did. A cotton rag rubbed with olive oil worked just fine to polish my wood furniture to a golden glow. A homemade mix of borax and washing soda replaced my phosphate-polluting dishwasher and laundry detergents. Soon I was switching to unbleached toilet paper and putting a commodious bin in the bathroom pantry for recycling.

I'm learning new tricks all the time. That's how green
cleaning works: One solution leads to another. There are
many points along the green continuum, each one
a different level of choice, knowledge, cost, and control.
This book tells you everything you need to know, and
gives you choices so you can decide what's right for your
lifestyle and your budget.

Nearly every commercial cleaner can be replaced with
safer, commonplace ingredients. It all starts with a
simple box of baking soda.

– Linda Mason Hunter

Why Clean Green?

Making the switch to a toxin-free, naturally clean home does great things for the environment — but it also makes you feel good. Your house will not only be clean; it will smell good, and it will reward you in subtle ways. You'll declutter your surroundings, making room for a new phase of life to unfold. You'll feel good about yourself, knowing you're doing your part to clean up the planet and make the world a better place for future generations. You'll provide an example for others, and learn a lot along the way. It may seem like a complex journey at first, but it is an attainable goal well worth the effort.

Think of your house as a second skin. If you nurture your physical body, keeping it tuned and healthy, you'll want to extend that TLC to your shelter, the four walls and roof surrounding you. Your home is an extension of yourself. It deserves to be healthy, too.

You don't have to change your home and your habits overnight. Achieving a truly healthy, green home is a gradual process, a series of little steps. And even the smallest changes make a difference.

The first step of green cleaning is commitment. Making a naturally clean environment takes mindfulness to each housekeeping decision. Your choices affect not only your home, but also those who live with you, the health of your community, and even the planet as a whole. Start by controlling the number of synthetic chemicals you use, eliminating this and minimizing that. Look for safer alternatives. Make compromises, if you must. When it comes to chemical cleaners, the milder the concentration, the lower the risk.

Cost should not be an obstacle. In many instances the green answer is the simplest and least expensive one. You'll soon discover that you don't need a closet full of specialized cleaning products. A half dozen may do the trick nicely.

You probably already have most of the basic ingredients for cleaning green in your kitchen and laundry room — baking soda, a couple of lemons, distilled white vinegar, salt, washing soda, pure soap, a few clean cotton rags. If making your own cleaners doesn't appeal to you, there are now scores of good environmentally friendly, nontoxic cleaners available at supermarkets, specialty shops, and online marketplaces. You won't have to worry about proper storage and disposal because these products aren't polluting at any stage of their lifecycle.

Like any commitment worth honoring, green cleaning comes with its own set of challenges. It takes awareness, education, experimentation, and a bit of elbow grease. But it's worth it. Along the way you'll learn that the quality of your life has little to do with using a harsh chemical to clean your toilet. By its very action, green cleaning says there is a better way.

What Is Green?

"Green" can mean a dozen different things to a dozen different people. For some, it means simply "environmentally friendly," no matter how vaguely that phrase can be used. In *Green Clean,* the word points to a deeper set of beliefs. By living green you seek to reduce your negative impact on the planet in small, everyday ways. It means treating all resources as precious; living with nature instead of trying to subdue it. It means being energy efficient, lessening your use of petroleum products, and conserving water. Most of all, it's a mindful way of living, trying to make every choice a green choice.

As defined by *The Green Consumer,* a green product is one that:

- is not dangerous to the health of people or animals;

- does not cause damage to the environment during manufacture, use, or disposal;

- does not consume a disproportionate amount of energy and other resources during manufacture, use, or disposal;

- does not cause unnecessary waste, due either to excessive packaging or to a short useful life;

- does not involve the unnecessary use of or cruelty to animals;

- does not use materials derived from threatened species or environments.

A Brief History of Housekeeping

Most homes may be clean, but very few of them are green. They're filled with a vast number of commercially made synthetic chemicals, all hiding in popular cleaners, polishes, pesticides, stain removers, and personal care products stored under the sink, in the basement, or in the garage.

Scientists at the National Toxicology Program found 5 to 10 percent of all chemicals in production could be carcinogenic in humans.

We've become dependent on these chemicals; the average American household uses 40 pounds of them each year. Whenever we have a housekeeping problem — whether a coffee stain or mold and mildew or a dirty kitchen floor — we often reach for a commercial product concocted in a laboratory, a brew of harsh chemicals designed to get the job done quickly but almost never gently or even safely. Cleaning product manufacturers have turned our near-obsession with cleanliness into an $18 billion industry that pollutes the environment, harms our bodies, and endangers future generations. How did things get so out of whack?

In the beginning, life wasn't easy, but it was simple. Humans lived in caves and hunted and gathered their food; trash went into a heap. Then, about ten millennia ago, the mighty agricultural revolution swept the planet. Shelter changed, too. Families began to live in huts made of wood, mud, stone, or the hides of animals. Housekeeping progressed — floors were swept, cobwebs whisked from corners, and hygiene became more important.

In the mid-1600s, the Western world entered the Industrial Age. The prosperity brought by this shift increased standards of living, and as houses grew larger, the task of housekeeping became more complex. By the mid-seventeenth century, spring house cleaning was a widely observed ritual — a week-long marathon in which house-keepers whitewashed walls, aired mattresses, blacked stoves, beat the dust out of rugs, oiled woodwork, and painted the rain barrel.

The Industrial Revolution, and the reforms that followed it, eventually caused epic shifts in the way people lived. By the beginning of the last century, changes in sanitation, agriculture, and general attitudes toward life led to a spectacular decline in mortality. Steel mills, textile factories, railroads, and food processing plants employed millions and brought goods and services closer to home. At home, indoor plumbing replaced outdoor privies; central heating replaced the wood or coal stove; electricity lengthened the productive hours of the day; and the hand-cranked washing machine, the icebox, and the gas oven simplified everyday chores.

Still, housekeeping solutions remained pretty simple. Through the 1930s, homemakers continued to make their own cleaners and stain removers from everyday ingredients — baking soda, distilled white vinegar, salt, lemon juice. World War II changed much of that. Chemicals initially developed for warfare found their way into America's cleaners, building materials, cosmetics, pesticides, and hundreds of other products. Advertisements promised to get clothes "whiter than white," make countertops "cleaner than clean," and bring "sparkle" to the toilet bowl. It was "better living through chemistry," as DuPont's slogan confidently declared.

Though most people weren't aware of it at the time, America's houses were filling up with fumes from paints, stains, cleaners, and other human-made materials. To make matters worse, we were becoming a "disposable society," encouraged by marketers to buy new, "improved" products every chance we got. Landfills burgeoned and burst, long before environmental safeguards were in place.

By the 1970s, the term "sick buildings" became a part of the lexicon, describing places where people reported an unusually high instance of symptoms like lethargy, fatigue, headaches, and nausea — all due to indoor air pollution. This was a result of poor design, bad ventilation, and a plethora of synthetic chemicals emanating ("outgassing") from furnishings and building materials and being sprayed into the air in the name of cleaning.

Housekeeping ain't no joke.

– Hannah, in
Little Women
by Louisa May Alcott

Our day-to-day habits have effects on our planet as well. In 2004 the World Wildlife Fund reported that human beings consume 20 percent more natural resources than the Earth can produce. The Clean Air and Water Acts and other environmental efforts have curbed a great deal of pollution, but chemicals still soil the Earth and its inhabitants. For example, dioxin, a known human carcinogen used for bleaching paper, is now found in the general U.S. population "at or near levels associated with adverse health effects," according to the U.S. Environmental Protection Agency (EPA).

Today, we are far more likely to breathe unhealthy substances inside our homes than outside. A five-year study by scientists at Harvard University, released in 1986 by the EPA, revealed that pollution inside the typical American home was two to five times worse than the air outdoors. We've insulated, caulked, and weather-stripped to the point where our houses no longer breathe. Unsafe chemicals hang around inside for days, creating a synthetic brew for us to inhale. The EPA continues to warn that indoor air pollution is a serious threat to human health.

Have nothing in your house that you do not know to be useful, or believe to be beautiful

– William Morris

A Chemical Legacy

More than 85,000 synthetic chemicals are in use today, and another 500 are added to the mix each year. Many of these new compounds are used to clean and sanitize our houses. No one knows what all the health consequences are of breathing these chemicals every day; the vast majority have never been tested for their effects on human health or on the environment. Because cleaning products are not reviewed before they come on the market, manufacturers respond to consumer complaints only after a product is on store shelves.

The human body can handle small amounts of poisons, but it begins to malfunction when burdened with toxic overload. Many chemicals are stored in body fat, while others migrate to vital organs, to the sheaths surrounding nerves, or to muscles, the brain, or spinal cord. Surely it's not coincidental that the increased use of manufactured chemicals coincides with a number of alarming health trends. For instance, breast cancer rates are 30 times higher in the United States than in less industrialized parts of Africa, while the incidence of asthma among preschool-age children has risen at least 160 percent since 1980.

These chemicals are produced in such huge amounts — and some have such long lives — that traces of them are routinely found in rain and snow, sediment, and surface waters. A 2003 study by the U.S. Geological Survey found low levels of household chemical compounds — including antibiotics, synthetic hormones, insect repellent, and an array of household cleaners — in 139 streams and rivers downstream from urban areas. Of the 95 chemicals found, 33 are known or suspected to be hormonally active; 46 are pharmaceutically active. These chemicals end up in wastewater treatment plants and, eventually, in our houses via kitchen and bathroom taps.

What's in My Cleaning Products, Exactly?

Since the ingredients of many household products are considered trade secrets, only the manufacturers know exactly what is in them. Consumers often have little to go on beyond mandated signal words like "danger," "warning," and "caution." These words, and longer warnings on some products, tell us what will happen with acute exposure, but nothing about long-term exposure. While some products present immediate dangers, such as drain cleaner and, for kids, dishwashing liquid, most chemicals are used a little here, a little there, week after week. Symptoms of chronic chemical toxicity appear over time and can include asthma; allergies; cancer; damage to the endocrine, immune, and nervous systems; reproductive and developmental disorders; organ damage; and the general condition known as multiple chemical sensitivity or environmental illness.

☠ **Warning Labels:** "POISON" and/or "DANGER" appear on substances that are extremely toxic, flammable, or corrosive. "WARNING" and "CAUTION" denote somewhat less hazardous substances.

Most of the chemicals found in household products fall into a few major classifications. Many products contain a mix of chemicals that cover more than one category.

Synthetic Organic Compounds
Some of these chemicals are building blocks for detergents and plastics, as well as for propane and other gas fuels, heating oil, and lubricants. They are common

in everyday household chemicals. Within this broad class you'll find:

Aromatic hydrocarbons: Many of these simple organic compounds are known to be carcinogens. They're used in degreasers, deodorizers, and pesticides.

Volatile organic compounds (VOCs): These chemicals evaporate easily at room temperature, then may attach to soft materials such as clothes, drapes, furniture, and carpeting. Eventually they dissipate into the outdoor air, where they cause low-altitude smog.

Petrochemicals: These compounds are linked to a host of environmental and health challenges, from oil spills and greenhouse gases to childhood developmental problems. The use of petrochemicals also reinforces our dependence on a dwindling supply of petroleum. The refineries that produce petrochemicals release some 492 million pounds of hazardous VOCs and 71 million pounds of air pollutants each year. They are found in a variety of household cleaners, including floor waxes, furniture polishes,

degreasers, and all-purpose cleaners. Watch out for the ingredients petroleum distillate and naphtha or naphthalene.

A New York Poison Control Center study found 85 percent of product warning labels to be inadequate.

Chlorinated Compounds

Chlorine is a highly toxic gas; one of its first uses was as a poison in World War I. Today there are some 15,000 chlorinated compounds in commercial use; some are found in common cleaning products, including sanitizing and bleaching agents, solvents (for dry cleaning, for example), tub and tile cleaners, and pesticides. Chlorinated compounds used in the home enter the environment when they get washed down the drain. Many of these chemicals are strikingly similar to human hormones and may be able to mimic them in the body; chlorinated compounds are suspected of affecting sperm counts, the rate of male births, and other biological functions.

Phosphates

Phosphates contain phosphorus, which acts as a nutrient in water systems. An overabundance of phosphorus encourages excessive growth of algae and weeds, robbing less aggressive plant and animal life of oxygen, resulting ultimately in lifeless streams and rivers.

Chemicals of Very High Concern

After a 2003 study of chemicals in household dust, Greenpeace compiled a list of "Chemicals of Very High Concern," including:

Alkyphenols: Found in some cosmetics and other personal care products, as well as in multisurface cleaners, liquid laundry detergent, paints, and floor coverings

Artificial musks: Found in cosmetics, shampoo, perfume, shaving foam, skin care products, liquid soap, air fresheners, laundry detergent, and dishwashing soap

Bisphenol A: Found in plastics, epoxies, and some skin care products

Brominated flame retardants: Found in mattresses, mattress pads, upholstered furniture, carpets, and some electronics

Chlorinated paraffin: Found in upholstered furniture, floor coverings, paints, plastics, and rubber products

Organotins: Found in shaving foam, floor coverings, carpets, pajamas, and air mattresses

Phthalates: Found in PVC plastics, including some children's teething and other toys; in shampoo, perfume, shaving foam, cosmetics, skin- and other personal-care products; shower curtains; air fresheners and multipurpose cleaners; and food packaging materials

Product	Health Risks
Aerosols	May contain propane and solvents. Many are combustible, posing a fire hazard. Aerosols release their contents in a fine mist, which hangs in the air and can be inhaled. Can irritate eyes and respiratory system.
All-purpose Cleaners	Many contain toxins that can be absorbed through the skin or by breathing. Many also contain synthetic surfactants, some of which may act as estrogen disruptors, contributing to gender abnormalities in animals and possibly in humans. May contain organic solvents, which are neurotoxins; benzene, a carcinogen; morpholine, which can cause liver and kidney damage; and butyl cellosolve, a nasal irritant and neurotoxin.
Antibacterial Soaps, Lotions, and Sprays	May contain pesticides, pesticide-like substances, and ammonia. Antibacterial compounds may encourage growth of antibiotic-resistant organisms.
Automatic Dishwasher Detergents	Often contain chlorine compounds and detergents with a high concentration of phosphates, which are harmful to waterways and fish.
Carpet Cleaners	**Extremely toxic to children.** May contain naphthalene, a member of the carcinogenic benzene family that is a neurotoxin and an eye, skin, and lung irritant. Can cause allergic skin reactions and cataracts; may alter kidney function.
Chlorine Bleach	**Chlorine is the chemical most frequently involved in household poisonings and is a potent environmental pollutant.** Chlorine (sodium hypochlorite) is part of a class of chemical compounds that may cause reproductive, endocrine, and immune system disorders. Chlorine degrades natural and synthetic fibers.
Degreasers	May contain kerosene, which can damage lung tissues and dissolve fatty tissue surrounding nerve cells.
Deodorizers, Air Fresheners	Contain chemicals that desensitize our noses; may contain naphthalene and formaldehyde, a carcinogen and respiratory irritant. Hazardous to the environment in manufacture and disposal and biodegrade slowly.
Disinfectants	May contain phenol, formaldehyde, cresol, ammonia, and/or chlorine, none of which kills all germs, either separately or in combination. Pollute indoor air during use as well as during storage if containers are not tightly closed. Can be harmful to internal organs and the central nervous system, and harmful to the environment during manufacture and disposal. See also Antibacterial Soaps.

Product	Health Risks
Dishwashing Liquids	**Dishwashing liquid is the most frequent cause of childhood poisonings.** Many are petroleum-based and nonbiodegradable and contain chemical additives for color and fragrance. They may contain cocamide DEA, a surfactant that can react with other compounds to form carcinogenic nitrosamines. See also Antibacterial Soaps.
Drain Cleaners	**Among the most hazardous products found in the home.** Usually contain lye and hydrochloric and sulfuric acid. Threaten the environment during manufacture and disposal.
Dry Cleaning	Toxic emissions from dry cleaning threaten workers, communities, and the environment. Fumes from dry-cleaned fabrics may pollute indoor air and enter our bodies.
Floor and Furniture Polishes	Can cause skin and eye irritation and central nervous system depression. Vapors can contaminate indoor air for days. Can contain cresol, amyl acetate, and petroleum distillates — all toxic chemicals hazardous to the environment in their manufacture and disposal. May contain benzene and organic solvents, which are neurotoxins.
Fragrances	Often made from petroleum-based chemicals. Many do not biodegrade. Can irritate skin, eyes, and allergies.
Glass Cleaners	Some contain ammonia, a poison that can irritate skin, eyes, and the respiratory system. May contain 1,4-dioxane, a probable carcinogen that is thought to suppress the immune system. May contain methanol, an acute toxin that can cause blindness.
Laundry Detergents	Some contain synthetic surfactants, which are slow to biodegrade and can release carcinogens and reproductive toxins during manufacture. May contain nonbiodegradable petroleum-based detergents. Artificial colors and fragrances may aggravate chemical sensitivities.
Metal Polishes	May release toxic fumes from a mixture of ammonia, phosphoric acid, and sulfuric acid. May contain fatty acid diethanolamines, which react with materials in the environment to form carcinogenic nitrosamines, and which may have hormone-disrupting effects.
Mold and Mildew Removers	Often an acute respiratory irritant. May contain chlorine and pesticides. May damage lungs, eyes, and skin.

Product	Health Risks
Mothballs	Often contain naphthalene and paradichlorobenzene, both toxic chemicals. Hazardous to the health of living things in their manufacture, use, and disposal. Children have confused mothballs for candy, resulting in seizures. Not readily biodegradable.
Optical Brighteners	These synthetic chemicals, found in many laundry detergents, convert UV light to visible light, making laundered clothes appear "white," but do not affect cleaning performance. Many are toxic to fish; do not readily biodegrade. Can cause skin allergy.
Oven Cleaners	**Among the most dangerous household cleaning products.** Can contain lye and sodium hydroxide — strong, caustic substances that cause severe corrosive damage to eyes, skin, mucous membranes, mouth, throat, esophagus, and stomach. Can be fatal if swallowed. Some contain benzene, a carcinogen.
Pesticides, Herbicides, Fungicides	**These are strong toxins, designed to kill.** They can contaminate indoor air and surfaces, posing a direct health threat to people and pets. They are also a threat to the environment during manufacture, use, and disposal.
Scouring Cleansers	May contain butyl cellosolve, a petroleum-based solvent that can irritate mucous membranes and cause liver and kidney damage. May contain crystalline silica, a carcinogen that is an eye, skin, and lung irritant.
Toilet Cleaners	**Among the most hazardous products found in the home.** Can contain chlorine and hydrochloric acid. Harmful to health simply by breathing during use. Fumes can escape even a closed container.
Tub, Tile, and Sink Cleaners	Can contain chlorine and may contribute to the formation of organochlorines, a dangerous class of compounds that can cause reproductive, endocrine, and immune system disorders. May contain phosphoric acid, which is corrosive in high concentrations, and is an eye, skin, and respiratory irritant.

Beyond Cleaning Green

Good planets are hard to find. We should do everything we can to minimize our destructive impact on this one. Green cleaning is a wonderful place to begin. Here are some suggestions for greening other areas of your life.

Become a Green Consumer

- Shop wisely: Buy green products whenever possible, avoid excess packaging, and look for biodegradable products.
- Take your own cotton or canvas bags to the grocery store.
- Replace your usual paper products with recycled ones, or use reusable products like cotton cloths instead of paper towels.
- Buy locally. It's good for your economy and saves energy in transportation.
- Replace your personal care products with green alternatives.

Maintain a Healthy Home

- Choose furniture made of natural fibers, whole wood, metal, and glass.
- Avoid using aerosols, such as hair spray and spray paint.
- Use low-VOC paints and low-VOC adhesives.
- Don't use chemical pesticides on your lawn or garden. Plan your landscape so it needs less chemical help — ask the staff at your local nursery for advice. If you have garden pests, call in an army of parasites and predators.
- Open up the windows and circulate fresh air through your house as often as possible.
- Have your air-conditioning and heating systems professionally inspected annually. Make sure your furnace, stove, and other combustion devices are vented directly to the outdoors.
- Select nontoxic bedding — most mattresses and bedding are made with a stew of chemicals, including chemical flame retardants and formaldehyde.

Conserve water. Fix leaky faucets and install low-flow toilets.

Become Energy Efficient

Turn down the heat at night to conserve fuel, or install a programmable thermostat.

Use compact fluorescent light bulbs.

Select a fuel-efficient, low-emissions car.

Walk or ride a bicycle instead of driving.

Community Action

Many household chemicals fall into the category of "suspected carcinogen." If you know a product contains toxic chemicals, vote with your pocketbook and don't buy it. Action is needed to keep these toxic chemicals out of consumer goods. Contact your representatives in Congress and tell them your concerns.

Help organize a neighborhood Dumpster day or large-item disposal day.

Promote recycling. Start a paint exchange with your neighbors, or organize a Zero Waste event. Check out the Zero Waste Campaign at *www. grrn.org/zerowaste.*

Contact a local environmental group and offer to work on local air and water pollution issues.

Start a community curbside composting program that sells compost to gardeners and nurseries.

Help make your community bicycle-friendly.

In the Workplace

Bring your green habits to the office. First steps include using less paper, recycling, and conserving energy and water. Talk to your facilities manager about nontoxic, environmentally friendly cleaning solutions. Two websites offering good ideas are *www.eya.ca/gwp* and *www.gov.ns.ca/enla/envin/p2/pdf/ g_office.pdf.*

2 : CLEANING GREEN

BEGINNING TO CLEAN GREEN IS NOT HARD. ALL YOU NEED TO DO IS TAKE ONE STEP. IT MAY BE AS SIMPLE AS BUYING A ROLL OF BLEACH-FREE PAPER TOWELS, FILLING A SPRAY BOTTLE OF CLUB SODA INSTEAD OF USING WINDOW CLEANER, OR ADDING A RECYCLING BIN TO YOUR HOME OFFICE. EVERY STEP YOU CAN TAKE TO CLEAN IN HEALTHIER, LESS

TOXIC WAYS WILL HAVE FAR-REACHING BENEFITS.

Cleaning green is about making changes, small or large, that together are good for your family, good for your community, and good for the environment. Figure out what you can do today, and jump in.

The Stages of Green

The prospect of cleaning green can be as intimidating as it is inviting. But with just a few simple steps, you can easily change the way you clean — and the way you think about cleaning.

Look at cleaning green as a series of stages, from beginner to advanced. Each stage contains actions and strategies that further your commitment to thoughtful housekeeping. They are small but powerful changes that will make a difference in the health of your family, your home, and the world around you.

Stage one involves small shifts in your cleaning repertoire. You might replace your conventional dishwasher detergent with a green alternative, for example, or install a clothesline instead of always using an energy-consuming tumble dryer. In stage two, you should be able to clean entire rooms — even the bathroom — with nontoxic products and with less waste. And in stage three, the scope of your activities will expand to include places like the garage and the garden.

Although the stages are progressive, you're not required to complete each stage or check off each strategy before moving on to the next. For example, making the shift to non-toxic cleansers doesn't have to mean making your own cleaning solutions from scratch — there are plenty of environmentally friendly store-bought products out there. Instead, look at the steps to cleaning green as possibilities to explore at your own pace, without fear of being judged or evaluated. Green cleaning is about being kind to yourself as well as to the environment.

STAGE 1

Begin the Process

Evaluate your cleaning cabinet.

Discard the most hazardous products in your home.

Stock your cleaning cabinet with safe, non-toxic products.

Set cleaning goals.

Stop wasteful cleaning habits.

Become a more active recycler.

STAGE 2

Deepen Your Commitment

Adopt new cleaning habits that reduce environmental impact.

Set up a recycling area.

Enhance indoor air quality with house-plants.

Add prevention to your tool kit — reduce the amount of cleaning that needs to be done.

Buy environmentally sound products in bulk.

Replace store-bought cleaning solutions with homemade ones.

Settle into a thoughtful, but comfortable clean-ing routine.

Bring an environmental mind-set to every clean-ing task, even the big ones.

STAGE 3

Beyond Simple Housekeeping

Tackle challenging areas such as the garage.

Monitor local air and water quality, and work in your community to make it safer.

Bring green cleaning ideas to your workplace and support recycling and other waste-reduc-tion practices there.

Organize community events such as clothing swaps and large-item recycling days.

Encourage others to join you in your green cleaning practice.

Why Green Cleaning Matters

The decision to adopt more thoughtful, healthful, and environmentally friendly cleaning practices is a reflection of values. Creating a green, healthy home means putting your and your family's well-being first, but it also reflects an awareness of how your household fits into a larger context. We choose to return to simpler formulas and tools, and we choose to act responsibly.

Turning these choices into concrete actions is the next step. The path to new green cleaning habits starts with choosing nontoxic alternatives to conventional household products. Green cleaning is simple, but powerful. By moving toward a more natural way of interacting with the world, you will signal to yourself and to others that we are not helpless in the face of environmental destruction. There is something each of us can do in our daily lives to make a difference — to, as Gandhi wrote, be the change we wish to see in the world.

Green cleaning is both intimate and global. It can transform your home into a place of comfort and health, but its reach is much greater than that. Cleaning green protects local waterways, soil, and landfill. When you reduce your environmental footprint by eliminating toxic chemicals and reducing the waste you create, you promote health for your entire community. When you purchase products manufactured by companies with good environmental business practices, you protect workers from being exposed to harmful chemicals.

Can all this good begin in our homes? Yes. When we change ourselves, we change everything.

Getting Started

There is no perfect prescription for cleaning green — just as there is no single best way to keep house. But having a plan is essential. In *Home Comforts*, a comprehensive guide to taking care of the home and everything inside it, Cheryl Mendelson notes that many of us approach housework without any system or routine, "more or less reacting to each situation as it arises. This makes things harder, not easier."

Green Clean is organized room by room; each chapter includes a checklist of tasks to take care of daily, weekly, monthly, and, occasionally, once or twice a year. Everyone's house is different, and you'll probably have things to add to the list. You don't have to become Martha Stewart, with a minute-by-minute schedule, but following a plan for your own house will help you keep it clean and orderly — and green.

A strategy should not be a burden. Setting reasonable goals and making adjustments to suit your needs and lifestyle will make your transition gentler. Consider the suggestions presented in *Green Clean* in light of your own comfort level and needs, and proceed at your own pace, creating your own approach. Your values will guide your choices as you begin your green cleaning practice.

When setting your cleaning goals, consider these questions: How much time do I wish to devote to cleaning? Do I require a continually spotless environment, or can I live with a more casual approach to cleanliness? Which parts of green cleaning appeal to me most?

The Tasks

The physical rituals of housekeeping — sweeping, dusting, scrubbing — are familiar ones. Most of us have been doing them in some form since childhood. But part of green cleaning involves stepping back and thinking through even these simple actions, and relearning the cleaning tasks we've grown up with.

Using safe, natural cleaning products — and using fewer products overall — is the first way these tasks change. Bend your knees to protect your back while damp mopping a floor. Be sure that you have a sturdy stepstool. Ask for help when you need it. A clean home is enjoyed by every member of the household, and every member can contribute to it.

Cleaning needn't be physically taxing. Green cleaning encompasses practices that will save time and conserve energy — not just the planet's, but your own.

Haste makes waste, no less in life than in housekeeping.

—— Henry David Thoreau

Out with the Old

The first step in green cleaning is to take a hard look at the cleaning products you use, then rid your house of the most toxic things in your cleaning cabinet. The Going Green chapter details some of the dangers inherent in many cleaning products; the chart on pages 21–23 is a quick reference to the worst offenders. (The Storage, Disposal & Recycling chapter has tips on how to safely get rid of these products.)

Some people will start with the products that are easiest to replace, like dishwashing liquid and all-purpose cleaner. Others will first focus on the most dangerous products, such as drain and oven cleaners. A simple rule of thumb for your cabinet clean-up: If something makes your eyes tear, your nose crinkle, or your skin itch, get rid of it. Almost every cleaning product can be replaced with a nontoxic, environmentally friendly alternative available at local stores or on the Web. It's also easy to make your own cleaning solutions from basic, safe ingredients — see the Recipes chapter. A combination of these approaches works great.

Cleaning up your cleaning cabinet will be a signal to your family that such items are no longer welcome in your home. The environment inside your home will be healthier, and your household will be helping to preserve the planet, even if it is one spritz at a time.

Restocking Your Cleaning Cabinet

There are thousands of conventional cleaning products out there — and hundreds more nontoxic, green alternatives. The first rule of making a green cleaning cabinet is that you don't need a different product for every cleaning task; green cleaning products are usually very versatile. A basic green cleaning kit — whether it consists of store-bought products or homemade solutions (see the Recipes chapter) — should include an all-purpose cleanser, a liquid soap, a nonchlorine bleach, and a heavier-duty cleaner for tough jobs.

When you're shopping for any type of cleaning product, read the label. Watch for federally mandated signal words — "poison," "warning," and "caution" — which indicate different levels of hazard, "poison" being the most dangerous. Chemically based commercial products almost never list their ingredients; to find out what's actually in them, visit the National Library of Medicine's Household Products Database at *householdproducts.nlm.nih.gov*.

On green cleaning products, look for the basics: "nontoxic," "biodegradable," "recyclable." (But note that these terms, as well as more generic words like "natural" and "environmentally friendly" have no legal definition.) You might also look for products that are free of dyes, fragrance, and phosphates.

Green cleaning products usually include a list of ingredients; such a list is a good way to know the manufacturer has nothing to hide.

Also consider the packaging. Can it be reused or recycled? Is it made of recycled materials? Is it excessive? To reduce waste, buy cleaning products in bulk, or in refillable bottles.

The Right Kind of Paper Towel

Look for paper towels and other paper products that are made of recycled paper and that have not been treated with chlorine bleach in their manufacture. To reduce waste, opt for reusable cloths or sponges over paper towels wherever possible.

The Three Graces: Baking Soda, Vinegar, and Soap

Throughout *Green Clean*, you will find recipes for simple home-cleaning preparations. The majority call for baking soda, distilled white vinegar, or liquid soap. These three nontoxic ingredients, singly and together, can deal with most household cleaning tasks.

 Baking soda is alkaline and therefore works well on acidic substances such as proteins, grease, and animal messes. It is slightly abrasive and can be used for scouring. It's also a natural deodorizer and grease cutter, and has mild bleaching properties. Some recipes may call for washing soda, which is a more alkaline (and more powerful) form of baking soda.

 Vinegar is acidic. It dissolves scale, inhibits mold, and cuts soap scum. For household cleaning always use plain distilled white vinegar. Vinegar works well on alkaline substances and stains such as coffee, rust, tea, and liquor.

If your home has hard water, which can lessen soap's effectiveness and create soap scum, you may want to invest in a water softener.

 Simple castile soap (made with olive oil) and vegetable-based soap (such as Murphy's Oil Soap) have a neutral pH. Soap cleans by attaching to soil at the molecular level, so that the soil can be rinsed away with water.

Tools for Cleaning

The right tools make cleaning easier and more efficient. Choose tools that are well made, and care for them properly. (A tool that lasts for years is an ecofriendly tool.) Store tools near where they are used, even if this means occasionally having multiples of the same item. A sponge, a small broom, and a small dustpan under every sink means that spills and accidents can be dealt with immediately. For those tools you wish to keep only one of, you may want to get a tool caddy or carrier so that you can reach for what you need as you move about the house.

Apron

An apron allows you to stow supplies and keep your hands free. Choose a sturdy cotton model with lots of pockets and keep it with your cleaning supplies.

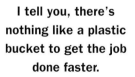

I tell you, there's nothing like a plastic bucket to get the job done faster.

– Eustace Conway, in
The Last American Man
by Elizabeth Gilbert

Broom and Dustpan

If possible, choose a broom made of natural broomcorn — it will last forever if you keep it from getting wet. You may want to have several brooms for different tasks. A stiff-bristled broom is best on rough or uneven surfaces, such as cement or stucco, while a broom with soft bristles works well on smooth surfaces, such as tile or linoleum. Angled brooms will help you to get at corners and baseboards. The best dustpans have a very thin edge and are long handled, so you don't have to bend down.

Bucket

The biggest mistake people make when buying a bucket is choosing one that is too big. A large bucket becomes too heavy and cumbersome to lift when it's full. Choose one that has an opening wide enough to accommodate your mop — often a square bucket will serve you better than a round model — and don't exceed a roughly ten-quart capacity. Make sure the handles are sturdy and won't cut into your hands.

Cloths

A good supply of cloths is invaluable. Make them from old cotton clothing or towels, or buy a pack. It's helpful to color-code them: green for dusting, red for wiping up spills, and so on. The best cloths are nonlinty fabrics such as flannel and cheesecloth. Absorbent fabrics such as terry are best for drying dishes. Launder cloths regularly and avoid using fabric softeners or other treatments, as their residue may interact with cleaning products or reduce absorbency.

Gloves

Natural cleaning formulas are less harsh than traditional products, but gloves are still necessary to keep your hands from drying out. Latex gloves are a good choice — they're biodegradable — but people with latex allergies will want to choose rubber, vinyl, or another alternative. Wash gloves in dish soap and dry them with a terry towel. Store them inside out.

Mop

Use a cellulose sponge mop, or a 100 percent cotton one.

Pumice Stone

Pumice, a natural abrasive, can be used to scrub away mineral deposits on toilets and other areas. Keep the pumice stone wet when you're scrubbing; you may want to test it on a small area to make sure it won't scratch your porcelain.

Scraper

A scraper is a wonderful tool for cleaning up hardened spills on walls, stoves, floors, and tile. Choose one that uses a single-edge razor blade and comes with a sturdy plastic holder and a cap for the blade. Use small strokes and always keep the blade pointed away from your body.

Scrub Brushes

Scrub brushes are great for when a sponge isn't strong enough for the job, especially for cleaning scummy tiles and other bathroom surfaces. Choose a natural-bristle brush with a wood handle.

Sponges

 It's good to have a variety of sponges for different tasks, and to keep them in the rooms where they will be used. Choose cellulose sponges whenever possible — they are biodegradable. Avoid those with antibacterial additives and chemical dyes. See page 51 for more information on sponges.

Squeegee

Squeegees make cleaning windows a much easier task and eliminate the need for paper towels or newspapers. An extendable handle lets you reach high windows.

Disposables

A number of cleaning tools with disposable cloths, pads, or brushes have recently arrived on the market. Avoid them. A lot of cleaning green is about being careful with what you use and how it's disposed of; disposable products create more waste by definition, they deliver chemicals straight into wastewater and landfills, and they consume excessive resources in their manufacture.

Toothbrush

 A toothbrush is great for scrubbing small and hard-to-reach spots, such as around faucets and in narrow spaces between tiles. If your home has a lot of tile, you may want to invest in a grout brush, too.

Vacuum

A vacuum cleaner is the best tool for getting dust and dirt out of carpets and upholstery, and regular vacuuming prevents dirt from being ground into your carpet and rugs. Choose the most powerful vacuum you can find, and one that is properly vented, has a HEPA filter, and comes with a full complement of accessories. If you aren't planning to get a new vacuum, consider switching to "micro-fine" or "micro-filtration" bags, which are better at trapping particles.

And as you sweep the room / Imagine that the broom / Is someone that you love.

– from "Whistle While You Work," in *Snow White and the Seven Dwarfs*

Making a Plan

No matter which stage of green cleaning you're in, choosing a starting point can be difficult. Each room of the house has daily, weekly, and monthly chores. The chore breakdowns that appear in the chapters that follow are just suggestions — you should plan your cleaning strategy based on your household's specific needs and your own cleaning goals. It may be helpful to make your own daily, weekly, and monthly lists. If more than one person in your home has cleaning responsibilities, divide up the tasks.

Your cleaning goals may vary from month to month or even day to day. Try to make yours realistic. Many of our cleaning standards have been shaped by commercial culture — they are often false ideals designed to get us to buy cleaning products. You may find, as your explore green cleaning, that these preoccupations fade and are replaced with a focus on the process of cleaning.

One way to start building your own cleaning system is to make a daily list, then go a week doing just the items on the list. At the end of a week, it will probably be clear that some tasks don't need to be done so frequently and can be moved to the weekly list. The next week, do your modified list and continue to shift tasks from daily to weekly, or vice versa, as needed. By the end of a month you should have a cleaning system that works for you and is flexible enough to be adjusted for houseguests, parties, and other special cleaning needs.

Daily maintenance — doing the dishes, sweeping or vacuuming, decluttering, making beds, and wiping down the shower or tub — ought not take more than 30 minutes total. Rather than a big weekly cleanup, you may wish to do some weekly tasks throughout the week. Monthly jobs —

flipping mattresses, washing walls and windows, vacuuming underneath furniture — may take an hour or more total, depending on how many people are helping.

Make Cleaning Fun!

Put on music that you enjoy, wear comfortable clothing, and take pride in your work. When you're done, take the time to admire your results.

Decluttering

Clutter not only makes it difficult to locate items when they are needed, it also interferes with cleaning because it obstructs surfaces. There are ways to manage clutter and keep it from getting out of control. A small library has already been written about getting your home organized; *Organizing Plain & Simple* and *Sink Reflections* are great books to start with.

Decluttering Tips

❀ Control clutter on a daily basis, before it becomes overwhelming.

❀ Declutter one room at a time. Don't move on to another task until the room is finished.

❀ Try to work in a clockwise sweep, so you don't miss any spots. (If you're left-handed, counterclockwise may work better.)

❀ Make each member of your household responsible for his or her own clutter.

❀ Having a bin for each family member in a hallway or entryway can speed decluttering of the house's main rooms. When you declutter, move each individual's belongings to the appropriate bin; each individual is then responsible for organizing or emptying his or her own bin.

3 : THE KITCHEN

THE GREEN CLEAN REVOLUTION BEGINS
IN THE KITCHEN. THIS IS THE CENTER
OF HOME LIFE, WHERE WE PREPARE
OUR FOOD, WHERE WE MEET BETWEEN
MEALS, AND WHERE WE GATHER WITH
OUR FAMILIES.

For all these reasons, it is important to establish and maintain a simple, healthful cleaning routine for your kitchen. Once you establish this flow, you'll have more time to spend with your loved ones. A commitment to nutritious food is enhanced by nontoxic cleaning practices. Simple things like a clean sink and shining floors make the whole house feel welcoming and provide peace of mind.

Many of us share a notion that the ideal kitchen is hyper-clean and industrially disinfected. We think that this kind of environment is the only one that can keep our families safe from food-borne illnesses — and we are sometimes willing to sacrifice our environmental principles in order to achieve this goal. But this is a false notion of cleanliness and healthfulness. That idealized, sterile kitchen is some-thing you see in a magazine, not in a home. A healthy kitchen is one that is lived in — a place where kids grab snacks after school, where you experiment with new recipes, and where lots of messy things happen. A clean and healthy kitchen is one that shines but doesn't rely on harsh detergents and cleaners to do so.

Getting Started

The first step in the kitchen, as in every room, is to take a hard look at the cleaning products you currently depend on. Almost every traditional, chemical-based product can be replaced — with a nontoxic, store-bought cleaner, or with an easy (really!) do-it-yourself solution. (See the Product Guide and Recipes chapter.) Start with dishwashing liquid and all-purpose cleaner, then move on to automatic dishwasher powder, specialty surface cleaners, stain removers, etc.

By eliminating toxic disinfectants and cleaning products, you'll greatly reduce the risk of accidental poisoning of children or pets — and limit your household's impact on the local water supply. Keeping a green kitchen means that the air in your home will be toxin-free, and that your meals will be made in a more healthful environment. Most of all, a green kitchen is one that has been thoughtfully cared for, one that reflects your values and your commitment to both family and community.

Clean Better

There are plenty of ways to minimize the stress of kitchen cleaning while still being green. Break the kitchen down into separate tasks and sort them by how often they need to be done (see chart, opposite). Try not to fall behind on the daily tasks — the weekly and monthly tasks will be easier, and you'll have less reason to be tempted by harmful, industrial-strength cleaning products.

Decluttering is a great way to start transforming your kitchen. Counters should be used as work space, not storage space. Appliances that aren't used daily should be kept under dust covers or in cupboards. Food that is stored in canisters should be in cupboards, the pantry, or the refrigerator. A decluttered kitchen feels cleaner and stays cleaner.

Consider investing in a cupboard organizer to maximize storage space. Consolidate items that are used together to save time throughout the day — cereal bowls near coffee cups, dinner plates near serving dishes. Items that are used rarely — holiday or party dishes, for example — can be stored in a

closet or the garage. As you begin to use environmentally friendly cleaning methods, you will need less space; simple natural products are more multifunctional than those from manufacturers who want to sell you a different product for each surface.

Some green cleaning practices will lead to new organizational schemes. For example, to reduce wasteful use of paper towels, you can use a variety of rags and sponges — one each for hands, dishes, floors, counters, appliances, and oven and stove cleaning. You can color-code them or give them separate, labeled hooks.

Kitchen Checklist

DAILY

- [ ] Load the dishwasher after every meal, and run dishwasher only when full.
- [ ] Hand wash items that aren't dishwasher-safe.
- [ ] Wipe down sink and countertops.
- [ ] Wipe fingerprints and smudges off cupboards, appliances, and walls.
- [ ] Clean stains and spills as they happen.
- [ ] Sweep the floor.

WEEKLY

- [ ] Discard food that is going bad.
- [ ] Damp mop the floor.
- [ ] Take out trash and recycling.
- [ ] Check and clear drains.
- [ ] Conduct pest control, if necessary.
- [ ] Beat or vacuum area rugs, if any.
- [ ] Wash sponges and rags.
- [ ] Clean coffee maker.

MONTHLY

- [ ] Clean the inside of the refrigerator.
- [ ] Clean oven.
- [ ] Clean dishwasher and check for scraps and blockages.
- [ ] Clean appliances.
- [ ] Dust light bulbs and lighting fixtures.
- [ ] Wax floors if necessary.
- [ ] Restock cleaning supplies as needed.
- [ ] Straighten cupboards.

Hand Washing Dishes

Washing dishes is a familiar daily task, and probably the first bit of housekeeping we learned to do. It's also one of the easiest to make more environmentally friendly and more efficient. Using a nontoxic, biodegradable dishwashing liquid, such as those from Ecover or Naturally Yours, is a simple first step. Avoid products labeled "detergent"; this indicates they are chemically derived. Making your own dish soap is another option — see Recipes, page 138. Pick up a natural sponge, like a cellulose sponge, a sea sponge, or a loofah, and you've detoxified your entire dishwashing process in two steps.

Try to wash dishes as soon as possible after meals. If you absolutely can't get to them right away, soak hard-to-clean items in hot water with a little baking soda. You can also sprinkle baking soda on pots or pans with burnt-on food and let them sit while you do the other items. But don't use baking soda on aluminum cookware — it can discolor the metal.

It's best to have two basins, one for washing and one for rinsing. If your sink has only one, use a dishpan for the rinse. Fill the first basin with hot soapy water, and the second (or dishpan) with very hot clean water. You only need about two tablespoons of dishwashing liquid. One to three tablespoons of distilled white vinegar in the rinsewater can help prevent spots if your home has

Sponge Options

Sea

Wood Brush

Cut Up Loofah

Cellulose

There are biodegradable alternatives to standard plastic sponges. The best choices are sea sponges (found at most natural food stores) and biodegradable cellulose sponges. A large, unused bath loofah cut into smaller pieces makes a good scouring pad; you can also use a wood scrub brush with stiff, natural bristles. To disinfect sponges and scrub brushes, wash them in soapy water, then place them in boiling water for three to five minutes.

hard water; a tablespoon also helps cut any grease in the rinsewater.

☠ Whichever dish-cleaning product you use, always store it out of reach of kids. Dishwashing liquid is a leading cause of accidental poisoning in small children.

Put the silverware in the bottom of the soapy water. Scrape any remaining food off the dishes into the trash or your compost bin and put the dishes on top of the silverware. Use a rag to wipe out greasy pots and pans and put them on the counter.

Wash glassware first, rinsing in the hot water, then china, and then silverware. Replace rinsewater when it cools or gets dirty. Pots and pans are next. Use a scouring pad or scrub brush and more dishwashing liquid if needed. It's best to let everything air-dry, with the exception of some glassware and crystal. If you can't wait, use a soft linen dish towel and dry items in the same order you washed them.

Dish racks get dirty, too — it's good to get in the habit of washing yours occasionally, just before or just after doing the dishes. Wash as you would a regular dish and make sure to let it dry thoroughly.

Glassware

Sparkling-clean crystal and glass-ware is one of the greatest joys of a dishwashing job well done. Even those who own automatic dishwashers often choose to hand wash such items to avoid spotting or scratching. Some tips for the best results:

- Wash glasses and crystal first, in clean, hot dishwater.

- Distilled white vinegar in your rinsewater prevents spotting; the mix can be up to one-third white vinegar for glassware.

- Slip glasses into hot water sideways to prevent cracking.

- Crystal should be hand dried and polished with a soft cloth.

- If your drinking glasses are cloudy, soak them for an hour or so in warm distilled white vinegar, then scrub.

To clean wax from crystal candlesticks, peel off as much as possible, then remove remaining residue using a cotton ball moistened with glycerin (available at most health food stores).

Cast-Iron

Cast-iron cookware is durable and efficient, and even adds a small bit of necessary iron to your diet. And using cast-iron cookware lets you avoid nonstick chemicals such as Teflon. A recent study showed harmful particles and gases were released from nonstick pans after just a few minutes on the stove top. Cleanup is easy, too: Use steel wool to scrub any stubborn stains, then rinse. Dry cookware over low heat to prevent rusting, and rub with vegetable oil to reseason. Do not soak cast-iron pots or pans.

Automatic Dishwasher

Using an automatic dishwasher can save hundreds of gallons of water when compared to hand washing — assuming you're doing full loads of dishes in a modern machine. Yours should be less than 10 years old; look for the Energy Star label, which ensures an appliance is energy-efficient.

Dishwashing Detergent

Until recently, it was a challenge to find an environmentally sound automatic dishwashing detergent. Traditional name-brand detergents (powders, liquids, and "tabs") contain both chlorine and phosphates. In fact, up to a third of the phosphates in U.S. wastewater comes from automatic dishwashing detergent. Phosphates are a major cause of algae blooms, which are hazardous to fish, plant life, and water quality. The ecofriendly dishwashing products listed in the Product Guide (see page 164) are all chlorine- and phosphate-free.

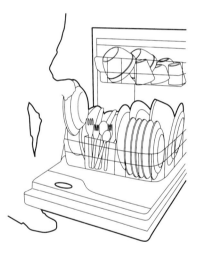

Loading the Dishwasher

Loading the dishwasher properly will save time and help conserve energy. Don't rinse dishes before putting them in the dishwasher — just scrape any food into the trash or composter. Prerinsing can be a hard habit to break, but it is almost always an unnecessary waste of time and water. Put the most soiled items, such as pots and pans with cooked-on food, on the bottom rack, facing down, so the sprayer arm will be pointed directly at them. Dishwasher-safe plastic-ware, glasses, cups, and mugs go on the top rack, with the glasses in the rows between the tines, not on them. Platters, cookie sheets, and trays go along the sides of the bottom rack, with dishes and bowls between these items and any pots or pans. Utensils go in the basket with handles down, except knives, which go in handle-up.

Running the Dishwasher

Try to run the dishwasher only when it is full — a full load uses less water and energy than two half-loads. Using it at off-peak hours can reduce your community's energy demands and keep your house cooler in the summer. Choose the economy cycle if your machine has one, and avoid the rinse and hold cycle. You don't need the drying cycle — just open the door and let the dishes air dry. (Remove glasses and wipe them with a dry soft cloth if you are worried about spotting.)

Maintaining your Dishwasher

Maintaining your dishwasher properly will keep it at peak energy efficiency. Once a month or so, check the drain and reservoir for food scraps, which reduce the dishwasher's effectiveness and create unpleasant smells. Keep the interior of the dishwasher clean by putting a cup of white vinegar in the detergent reservoir and running an empty cycle every week or two. A little baking soda sprinkled on the floor of the washer prevents odors between uses.

Caring for Your Sink

Once the dishes are taken care of, cleaning the sink itself is easy. Still, it's important to avoid using anything toxic in or around the sink, as everything that goes down the drain can eventually enter the local water table. Many municipal water treatment facilities fail to sufficiently remove toxins.

Stainless Steel

For stainless steel sinks (and stainless steel dishwashers and refrigerators), use a nontoxic all-purpose cleaner, or try full-strength distilled white vinegar on a sponge. Never use abrasive cleaners or steel wool. If a spot needs scrubbing, use a little baking soda on a damp sponge. (Always scrub with the grain on stainless steel.) Rust stains can be removed by rubbing with a paste of two parts baking soda to one part water, then rinsing well.

Porcelain

Baking soda on a damp sponge also works for porcelain sinks. As with stainless steel, avoid abrasive cleaners. An ecofriendly cream cleanser or a nontoxic, nonabrasive cleaner like Bon Ami will help with any difficult stains.

Chrome

Chrome faucets and fixtures can be cleaned with a little club soda, a solution of equal parts distilled white vinegar and water, or a nontoxic all-purpose cleaner. If they are very grimy, try putting a few drops of a citrus essential oil on your cleaning toothbrush and scrub.

☼ To keep a garbage disposal sweet-smelling, grind up some ice cubes with lemon or grapefruit peels every week or so.

Give Your Sink a Bath

If a porcelain sink — in the kitchen or the bathroom — becomes scuffed or stained, try an herbal bath. Steep several bunches of rosemary or thyme in hot water for a few hours, then strain. Stop up the sink, pour the mixture in, and let it sit overnight.

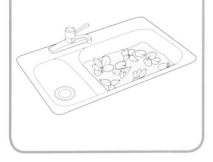

Taking Care of the Drain

Drain cleaners are among the most dangerous household products. (See page 22 for a rundown of how they can be harmful.) The best way to avoid using caustic drain cleaners is to prevent clogs and buildups in the first place. Scrape dishes well before you put them in the sink, use a trap or screen to keep food scraps out, and don't pour your cooking grease or oil down the drain. Grease builds up in your pipes and your community's pipes, eventually blocking them and causing sewer leaks and spills. Instead, allow the grease or oil to cool and collect it in a sealable container, then throw it away or compost it. A few cities offer grease and oil recycling, and a local restaurant may be able to include your household grease in their commercial recycling.

Once a week, pour a kettle of boiling water down the drain to flush it out. If the drain does become clogged, use a plunger, or try the DIY recipe, opposite. New enzyme-based drain cleaners (see Product Guide, page 168) break down organic matter that clogs drains; they work overnight, don't use caustic chemicals, and are safe for septic systems. For stubborn clogs, using a plumber's snake — or just calling a plumber — is a good choice.

Make Your Own Drain Opener

Add one cup baking soda and one cup vinegar to a large pot of boiling water (they'll fizz) and pour down the drain; the combination will dissolve fatty, greasy clogs. Flush with tap water until it clears.

Countertop Cleaning

For basic daily cleaning of most countertops — including laminate and Corian surfaces — use a simple mixture of vinegar and water, one of the all-purpose cleaners in Recipes (page 136), or an eco-friendly store-bought cleaner. If you have a stubborn stain or spot, make a baking soda paste (mix three parts baking soda to one part water), apply it, and let it sit for a few hours, then wipe and rinse.

Avoid products with the words "antibacterial" or "disinfectant" on the label — these can be toxic. "Antibacterials" can increase microbe-resistance on a large scale, and an all-purpose cleaner will do the job just as well.

A bit of baking soda on a damp sponge can clean most countertop stains. Keep a small bowl of baking soda near the sink for this purpose.

If you have marble counters, don't use anything acidic on them (lemon or vinegar, for example); it will corrode the surface. Instead, use a solution of one tablespoon dishwashing liquid in a quart of warm water. Rinse well to remove soap, and then dry with a soft cloth. Don't let marble air dry; it can spot easily.

Refrigerator and Freezer

Refrigerators usually use more energy than any other appliance. There are several strategies that will increase their efficiency. First, keep the refrigerator clean — it runs more efficiently that way. To clean the inside of the refrigerator and the freezer, use a nontoxic all-purpose cleaner, or try a mixture of four tablespoons baking soda in one quart of water. If there are spots that resist an initial pass, put straight baking soda on a damp sponge and scrub. The coils behind or underneath the refrigerator tend to collect dust and should be cleaned periodically to keep them working efficiently — use a coil-cleaning tool or a simple feather duster.

☼ Label fresh food with its purchase date and containers of leftovers with their storage date. Use the older items first to reduce waste and spoilage.

Don't overload the refrigerator — cool air needs to be able to circulate around and between items for the machine to do its job. The door racks are the warmest spot; use them to store things that won't easily spoil, like condiments.

A Sweet-Smelling Fridge

The classic box of baking soda in the fridge (and freezer) still works, but there are other ways to absorb odors: **(1)** Fill a plastic tub with active charcoal (from a pet store), poke holes in the lid, and seal it tightly. **(2)** Leave a half-cup of ground coffee in a bowl on a center shelf for a few days. **(3)** If you're deodorizing after cleaning out the refrigerator, try leaving a bowl of clay cat litter inside the empty fridge for 24 hours.

Oven and Stove Top Care

Ovens have acquired a reputation for being difficult to clean. But commercial oven cleaners have become increasingly toxic, with labels that warn about even touching the contents. This level of chemical concentration is unnecessary — and it can transfer toxins to your food. With typical use (or a self-cleaning oven), you shouldn't need to resort to any hazardous products to maintain your oven. A few preventive measures, simple maintenance, and the occasional deep cleaning with an eco-friendly formula will be enough.

When stove-top spills occur, try to wipe them up with a damp cloth or sponge before they get cooked on. If they're past that point, scrub with a nontoxic nonabrasive cleanser or baking soda paste — you might want to soften the area first with some hot water. Your weekly cleaning routine should include washing drip pans, oven racks, burners or rings, knobs and handles, and the exterior of the stove.

Ideally, you should wipe down the oven after every use with a non-toxic store-bought cleaner or with full-strength distilled white vinegar. If, like most people, you can't get to cleaning the oven every day, try to do it at least weekly to avoid stain and spill buildup, and after cooking anything that could have splattered. Cover fresh spills with salt — the food will be absorbed by the salt, which can then be easily scraped off. Self-cleaning or continuous-cleaning ovens rarely need more than this.

> ☼ **Lining the oven, broiler, and burners with foil only takes a minute and eliminates the need to deal with most spills, drips, and splatters.**

Other Appliances

Appliances make our lives easier, but they aren't always easy to clean. A few simple tricks can make upkeep a snap.

Storage

If you've decluttered (see page 48), then you keep the appliances you don't use daily stored in a cupboard or pantry. These items should be cleaned immediately after use, then returned to their storage spot. More frequently used appliances should be wiped after use or when they acquire fingerprints, and parts that come into contact with food should be cleaned along with the dishes. (See opposite page for more specific instructions.)

Cleaning

The outside of most appliances can be cleaned with club soda, a DIY all-purpose cleaner (see Recipes, page 136), or a store-bought all-purpose cleaner — look for one that says it is appropriate for use on appliances. Make sure to unplug appliances before cleaning.

Food residue can cling to can openers, both electric and hand-operated models. Wipe yours clean after every use, and clean regularly with a toothbrush dipped in baking soda. Nonelectric openers can go in the dishwasher.

No More Paper Filters

Permanent coffee filters, made of a fine-mesh metal, last for years. This saves paper, and means that less of the chemicals used in filters' manufacture will be returned to the environment. You can wash metal filters by hand, with soap and water, or on the top shelf of a dishwasher. French-press coffee makers also take paper filters out of the picture.

BLENDER

Make a "soapy shake" by filling the blender halfway with warm water, adding a drop of dishwashing liquid, and then running on low. Rinse well.

COFFEE GRINDER

Wipe out the interior and the burs after each use with a soft cloth. Wash the top as you would a dish, once a week.

TOASTER OVEN

It's very important to keep the oven tray clean in order to prevent fires. Line it with foil and re-place the foil weekly, or wipe it out after use (and cooling) with a damp sponge or cloth.

COFFEE MAKER

Clean the glass carafe after every use as you would a dish — other-wise oils can build up and cause the coffee to become bitter. Once a week, run a cycle with white vinegar instead of water (and with no coffee), then follow that with three or four cycles of hot water.

FOOD PROCESSOR

Wash dishwasher-safe parts in the dishwasher or by hand. Wipe the rest with white vinegar or an all-purpose cleaner.

MICROWAVE

Try to wipe up food spills and splatters as they happen. A good weekly cleaning will take care of the ones you don't catch right away: Put one cup water and two table-spoons baking soda in a bowl and microwave on high for two to three min-utes in order to soften any hardened food and to eliminate odors. Then wipe interior clean with diluted dishwashing liquid and rinse well.

TOASTER

Turn it upside down over a trash can and shake out crumbs (or pull out and empty the crumb tray). Clean the exterior with window cleaner or with nontoxic all-purpose cleaner (if toaster is plastic) or with club soda (if toaster is chrome).

Floors

The best practice for maintaining a clean floor is to wipe up spills as they happen, sweep daily, and damp mop weekly or as needed. For spills that leave a stain, refer to the Stain Guide. Most floor waxes and wax strippers contain VOCs and other hazardous chemicals. These products should be replaced with commercial nontoxic versions, or with simple, homemade solutions (see Recipes, page 140).

Get rid of the Dustbuster and rediscover your broom. As a daily task, sweeping can provide a valuable quiet moment as well as the satisfaction of a job well done. Sweeping will also remove abrasive soil that can scratch the floor. Begin in a corner and work your way around the room's perimeter, making sure to get the baseboards. Continue sweeping toward the center, and then pick up the dust and dirt with a dustpan. (If you use a vacuum cleaner, your path should be the same.)

Damp mopping should be done weekly or whenever dirt or stains build up. Always sweep before damp mopping. For most floors, you can use the basic floor cleaner described in the Recipes chapter or a non-toxic store-bought cleaner; or try a solution of a quarter cup castile soap in two gallons of warm water. If the floor is greasy, add a quarter cup vinegar. Fully soak the mop in the bucket of cleaning solution and wring it out over the sink. Mop from one end of the room to the other, without mopping yourself into a corner. Wring and resoak the mop as necessary — a dirty floor demands much more cleaning solution. If your no-wax floor looks dull, it may be soap buildup — try mopping with a solution of a half cup white vinegar in two gallons of water.

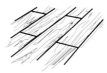 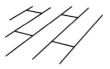

SEALED HARDWOOD FLOORS

Wood floors with polyurethane or other finishes are very low-maintenance. Don't wax these floors; just sweep and damp mop, going with the grain of the wood. Polish with a dry terry cloth if you desire a high shine.

UNSEALED WOOD FLOORS

Sweep, then apply raw linseed or jojoba oil bimonthly with a mop reserved exclusively for this purpose. Let the oil sink in, then dry mop. Try to keep water away from unsealed wood.

PAINTED WOOD FLOORS

After sweeping, damp mop weekly with highly diluted dish soap or the homemade floor cleaner described in Recipes, page 140. Don't use a cleanser containing pine oil on painted floors; it can damage the paint.

CERAMIC TILE

Don't use soap on tile floors. Instead, mop with a solution of half distilled white vinegar and half water or a nontoxic commercial floor cleaner recommended for this purpose. If it seems dull, polish with a dry terry cloth — there is no need to use any polish if you've mopped. Be especially vigilant about sweeping tile floors in the summer, when sand and dirt can get tracked in and scratch them.

STONE

Don't use soap here, either. Try a solution of two tablespoons washing soda in two pints water.

Putting a small, rubber-backed rug in areas prone to spills and spots, like in front of the sink and stove, can save time spent cleaning floors. Launder along with your kitchen towels.

Walls

In addition to collecting fingerprints and food stains, kitchen walls can also develop a greasy buildup from cooking — and then dirt will cling to that grease. Cleaning walls once a week is usually enough. If your kitchen is wallpapered, you might want to dust once or twice during the week, too — wallpaper attracts dust.

Clean walls from top to bottom, using a sturdy stepladder to reach upper areas. For painted walls, use a nontoxic all-purpose cleaner or make a solution of equal parts vinegar and water; spray and then wipe with a cloth or a sponge. If your walls are especially greasy, add a few drops of eucalyptus or spearmint essential oil to the spray bottle.

There are three basic types of wallpaper: plain paper, which is rare today; washable wallpaper, which has been coated with plastic; and "scrubbable" wallpaper, which has a vinyl coating. Plain paper wallpaper is quite delicate. Use a dry sponge and dust carefully. Washable wallpaper and scrubbable wallpaper can be cleaned with the same solution used on painted walls.

For greasy stains on walls, apply some baking soda paste and let it dry, then brush off. This same method should work for crayon marks. For other stains, see the Stain Guide.

Never use a cleaner containing pine oil on painted walls — it can act as a solvent on the paint.

Wood Walls
See the previous page for strategies to deal with most types of wood surfaces. If the wood is unfinished, use raw linseed oil to clean it, and try to keep water off it. But use linseed oil sparingly — it dries slowly and can encourage mildew.

Dealing with Food

Lowering the risk of food contamination, spoilage, and poisoning begins with good handling practices. Wash your hands before and after touching foods; if you have cuts or scratches on your hands, wear gloves. Keeping food from spoiling is much more important than disinfecting kitchen surfaces. "If you are worried about food poisoning," according to a recent *New York Times* story, "the best defense is the refrigerator."

Use one cutting board for meats, one for everything else. Wood cutting boards are preferable; your knife will tear up a plastic board, providing places for food-borne bacteria to thrive. (The surface of wood boards is a hostile place for most food-borne bacteria.)

A cutting board that has been used to cut bread, cheese, or vegetables can be cleaned with dishwashing liquid, or by sprinkling it with baking soda and then scrubbing it clean with a damp sponge. You can also sprinkle it with salt, then scrub it with a halved lemon. Sterilize a cutting board used for meat by putting it in the sink and pouring boiling water over it, then scrubbing it clean with soap and hot water.

Treat wood cutting boards with mineral oil once a month, to prevent it from drying out.

☼ Clean your sponges regularly by washing them in soapy water, then dropping them into boiling water.

Washing Produce

Fruits and vegetables are often covered with pesticides, herbicides, fungicides, or wax. Wash produce just before use, not before storing, which can make it go bad faster. For firm-skinned produce, you only need a little warm water and a scrub brush. Rinse well. Soak soft produce, such as strawberries, for a minute in plain water.

Pest Control

Where there is food, there are bound to be pests. While it's never pleasant to discover these visitors, it's comforting to remember that insects, mice, and the like are a part of the natural world, and their presence in our homes should not be taken as a sign of moral failing. That said, there are many safe ways to rid our houses of them.

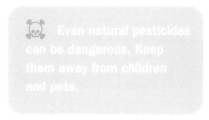

☠ Even natural pesticides can be dangerous. Keep them away from children and pets.

The least toxic way to deal with pests is to discourage them from entering your home in the first place. First, defend the perimeter: Check your baseboards, the backs of cupboards, crawl spaces, and other spots that might be used to gain entry. Block holes and cracks as tightly as possible. The best store-bought caulking choice is 100 percent silicone. You can also use linseed oil putty. Steel wool works well for keeping rodents out. Second, make your home as unwelcoming an environment for pests as possible: Clearing out clutter and maintaining a clean kitchen are matters of health as well as aesthetics.

Mice and Rats

The traditional, and still effective, way of dealing with rodents is to get a cat or a dog that will go after them. (Terriers are known for rodent-catching.) Mice hate peppermint, so putting peppermint essential oil wherever you find their droppings can be an effective technique. Try making a spray with two tablespoons castile soap, 20 drops peppermint oil, and a gallon of water. Humane (catch-and-release) traps are available at most hardware stores, but this method will only work if the population is small. Traditional snap-traps provide a quick kill; glue traps and poisons should be avoided.

Flies

Flies don't like basil, so this herb forms the basis of most non-toxic fly repellents. For fruit flies, try a spray of two teaspoons basil essential oil (find it at a health food store) in two cups water. You can also put several basil plants around the kitchen — the herb is easy to grow, fragrant, and can also be used in cooking.

Ants

Ants hate cinnamon and cayenne pepper. Sprinkling either along their suspected path of entry will repel them. You can also mix the cinnamon with some dishwashing liquid to make a paste and spread it along entryways. Or, make nontoxic ant traps by mixing one cup borax, one cup sugar, and three cups water. Soak a wad of paper towel or toilet paper in the mix, then put it in a small glass jar with a metal lid, like a baby food jar. Pierce the lid a few times with a nail, then place in any areas with an ant problem.

Cockroaches

Cockroaches love water, so check your home for leaks and wipe the sink dry after use. Sprinkle a mixture of sugar and borax near their trail — they will eat it, return to the nest, and die. Or spread Epsom salts, which irritate and repel them. There is also a commercially available, pesticide-free roach trap; visit *www.pestproducts.com* for information.

Although the goal of *Green Clean* is to help make a toxin-free home, we recognize that some stubborn roach infestations require the use of roach baits, like Combat brand traps, which have proven very effective, have no odor, and let you avoid spraying pesticides in your home. Use them according to the package instructions.

For a good all-purpose insect repellent, try a teaspoon each of eucalyptus and pennyroyal essential oils in two cups water. Spray along baseboards and other areas of infestation.

4 : THE BATHROOM

THE BATHROOM MUST BE MORE THAN CLEAN — IT MUST ALSO BE A SANCTUARY. WE RETREAT TO THE BATH TO RELAX AND TO REJUVENATE OURSELVES. FOR THESE REASONS, A CLEAN, HEALTHY, TOXIN-FREE BATHROOM IS ESSENTIAL. YET, STORED BENEATH THE BATHROOM SINK, WE FIND DANGEROUS CHLORINE BLEACH, HARSH CLEANERS, AND UNNECESSARY

FRAGRANCE PRODUCTS. USING NATURAL PRODUCTS AND STICKING TO A SIMPLE ROUTINE WILL NOT ONLY PREVENT HARM- FUL SUBSTANCES FROM AFFECTING LOCAL ECOSYSTEMS, BUT ALSO PROTECT OUR FAMILIES FROM REPEATED EXPOSURE TO FUMES, SKIN IRRITANTS, AND ALLERGENS.

O! Water hot is a noble thing.

– J.R.R. Tolkien,
Bilbo's Bath-Song

Getting Started

Bathrooms are particularly susceptible to mold, mildew, and harmful bacteria — all of which thrive in damp, warm environments. Many people believe that only industrial disinfectants, chlorine bleaches, and other dangerous chemicals can get a bathroom truly clean, but this simply isn't the case. Even the harshest chemicals won't give you a sterile environment; there will always be some bacteria present. More important, it's just as easy to keep the bathroom clean with safe products.

Traditional disinfectant products have noxious environmental effects. Typical ingredients, such as sodium or potassium hydroxide, sodium hypochlorite, and hydrochloric acid, are highly caustic and dangerous to handle or inhale. Furthermore, they may contribute to the rise of drug-resistant bacteria and cause elevated estrogen levels in wildlife when they are added to our water supply — which is what happens when you wash them down the drain. Plant-based cleaners and essential oils with antiseptic properties are smart alternatives that will destroy microbes without causing harm to the environment.

The best way to deal with mold and mildew is to prevent them from gaining a foothold. Mold spores are always around, in the air and on surfaces throughout the house. It's only when they get out of control that they become a problem. Keep surfaces dry and allow air to circulate through the bathroom as much as possible — this will help with odors, too. Open a window, use the ceiling fan (install one, if necessary), or purchase a small fan to put on the countertop. Also, make sure your pipes aren't leaky and that your toilet doesn't sweat onto nearby walls — any excess moisture will help mold and mildew grow.

Even with such moisture-control efforts, keeping your bathroom 100 percent mold- and mildew-free can be difficult. But beware the plethora of mold and mildew cleaners that have come to market in the past few years. These solutions are highly concentrated with many toxins, including chlorine, formaldehyde, and sodium hypochlorite, which irritate your eyes, lungs, and skin. Using them in the confines of the bathroom puts your and your family's health at risk and should be strictly avoided if anyone in the home has asthma or other chronic health problems. (The *Wall Street Journal* likened one leading brand's smell to "a noxious swimming pool" and reported that the product made eyes tear, "even in a well-ventilated bathroom.") When these chemicals go down your drain they can react with others and form dangerous compounds like chlorine gas.

There are effective, nontoxic alternatives to these products — though they can require a bit more elbow grease, and they can sometimes have less shiny results, since they don't use chlorine bleach. Look for ingredients like borax, hydrogen peroxide, tea tree oil, and pine oil — all are good, nontoxic mold and mildew fighters. See the Product Guide for recommended cleaners (page 167), or try the do-it-yourself treatment below.

DIY Mold and Mildew Treatment

A spray made from one drop of tea tree oil to one cup of water will help clean up most mold and mildew problems. Keep the solution handy in a spray bottle; it should last for months. A simple vinegar spray (a half cup distilled white vinegar to one cup water) is also effective and has a less intense scent.

Bathroom Checklist

DAILY

- [ ] Wipe sink after use.
- [ ] Wipe shower and/or tub after use.
- [ ] Hang up towels to dry.
- [ ] Deal with stains as they happen.

WEEKLY

- [ ] Sweep or vacuum and damp mop.
- [ ] Vacuum rugs.
- [ ] Clean the toilet, sink, and tub.
- [ ] Clean mirrors and countertops.
- [ ] Launder towels and washcloths.
- [ ] Empty trash and recycling.
- [ ] Clean windows.
- [ ] Clean walls as necessary.

MONTHLY

- [ ] Maintain drains.
- [ ] Clean window curtains or blinds.
- [ ] Clean grout.
- [ ] Clean and organize cabinets.
- [ ] Dispose of old medications.
- [ ] Launder shower curtain.
- [ ] Wash bathroom rugs.
- [ ] Address mold and mildew, if necessary.

For everyday bathroom cleaning, a nontoxic all-purpose cleaner might be all you decide to use, although there are many specialized formulas for mirrors, toilets, faucets, tiles, and other surfaces. During a weekly cleaning, it's best to clean the bathroom in a circular path, going from fixture to fixture, then spot cleaning walls and, finally, sweeping and damp mopping floors.

Don't beat yourself up if you find the transition to a naturally clean bathroom challenging. Try incrementally reducing the amount of chemical cleansers and gradually work your way up to a wholly green cleaning practice.

Bathroom Tools

Plunger

Plungers are a simple, nonchemical way to unclog toilets and drains. Look for the type with an extended "plug"—they create a better seal. Position the plunger over the opening as tightly as possible and push down. Wait a few seconds, then pull the plunger up. It may take several tries to flush a stubborn clog — start with gentle pushes then gradually add intensity and reduce the wait time. After use, sterilize the plunger by pouring boiling water over it.

Pumice Stone

A soft pumice stone is useful for scrubbing away mineral deposits and stains on marble.

Snake

Snakes (sometimes called augers) are more versatile than plungers but can be messier and more difficult. Snakes probe your pipes until they penetrate and break up the clog so it can be flushed away. As with plungers, it may take several tries. There are professional-grade powered snakes available, as well as hand-cranked and drill-powered models. Follow the manufacturer's directions; wear grippy gloves because the snake can become wet and dirty. After use, sterilize the snake with boiling water and let dry thoroughly before storing.

Squeegee

A small squeegee makes a wonderful tool for cleaning shower enclosures and tiling. Small squeegees are available at home-supply and automotive stores.

Toilet Brush and Swab

Both of these tools make it easier to clean the toilet bowl and rim. A brush is more effective at dislodging scum and scrubbing away mineral deposits. Look for one with stiff natural bristles. Toilet swabs are handy cleaners and can also be used to lower the water level in the toilet bowl so it can be cleaned more easily.

Toilet

Cleaning the toilet doesn't have to be an unpleasant task. It's important not to get behind, as the unpleasantness increases over time. With the proper tools and cleaners, toilet cleaning and maintenance can be, if not fun, less of a burden.

Most commercial toilet cleaners contain dangerous acids, bleaches, or other toxic agents, including hydrochloric acid and hypochlorite bleach. You will see large cautionary labels on these products that explain how to avoid harming yourself when using them. The best way to reduce that risk is to avoid using them altogether. Simple, green alternatives will get the job done without polluting your home or your local water supply.

Clean the bowl first. Lift the lid and squirt your toilet bowl cleaner around (see the Product Guide, page 167, and Recipes, page 144); you might also try using an all-purpose cleaner rather than a specialized product. (Toilet bowl cleaners differ from other cleaners primarily in that they are generally thicker, so they'll cling to the sides and the rim. They may also contain special ingredients to fight scum and scale.) Make sure to apply the cleaner up under the rim. Your cleaning will be more effective if you use a toilet swab and empty the bowl of water first (see Bathroom Tools, opposite). Let the cleaner sit and work while you clean the outside of the toilet.

☼ Flushing the toilet with the lid closed releases less moisture into the air, keeping the bathroom less damp and thus helping limit mold and mildew.

Spray an all-purpose cleaner all over the toilet exterior and wipe with a soft sponge or cloth. Next, scrub the toilet bowl and flush. If the bowl has a ring of mineral deposits, try scrubbing them lightly with a pumice stone or applying some distilled white vinegar with a toilet brush or a sponge.

☼ One flush can use up to seven gallons of water. Encouraging your family to flush less often can result in significant water savings.

Air fresheners

No one wants a bad-smelling bathroom — an entire industry has developed around our fear of bathroom odors. Most commercial air fresheners simply add fragrance and oil to the air, masking smells and introducing chemicals to our indoor environment. Commercial deodorizers may contain carcinogens like formaldehyde and neurotoxins such as naphthalene.

Toilet Paper

Toilet papers are often made with chemical fragrances, dyes, softening agents, and harsh bleaches. Choose a paper product made from recycled pulp that has not been bleached or processed with chlorine bleach. (When chlorine is used in paper processing, dioxins and organochlorides are released into wastewater. Paper processing is the leading cause of chlorine contamination in the environment.) Products may be marked TCF, PCF, or ECF. TCF, or "Totally Chlorine Free," means the product is new, unrecycled paper that has not been bleached or processed with chlorine or chlorine derivatives. PCF, or "Processed Chlorine Free," paper is recycled and no chlorine has been used since it was reclaimed. ECF, or "Elemental Chlorine Free," paper has been processed with a chlorine derivative, making it the least green choice.

There are many simple, natural ways to improve bathroom air quality. Air circulation is important: Keep windows and doors open as much as possible. Use the bathroom fan if you have one. Instead of masking odors, absorb them. An open box of baking soda or a muslin bag filled with clay kitty litter are both effective options. You can also make an air freshener by combining two cups of hot water, a teaspoon of baking soda, and the juice of one lemon. Let the baking soda dissolve, pour the mixture into a spray bottle that produces a fine mist, and spray.

There are also plant-based air fresheners available; choose a biodegradable, non-aerosol formula in a recyclable container. If you prefer your bathroom to have a slight fragrance, try burning incense or a scented soy-based candle. There are also several types of essential oil diffusers available.

Light a match — it's the oldest trick in the book. Leave an open matchbook on top of the toilet for guests.

Bathtub and Shower

It's ironic that the spot where we go to get clean can get so
dirty. Nevertheless, the bathtub and shower require regular
upkeep, as soap scum and mildew will quickly accumulate if
they are neglected.

There are specific products available for grout, porcelain, fixtures, shower curtains, tiles, and more. However, you can probably use a simple nontoxic all-purpose cleaner and just a couple of specialized products, depending on your needs and cleaning goals. Homemade cleaners work well, too; see Recipes, page 136.

To clean tile walls and enclosures, spray a nontoxic all-purpose cleaner or tile cleaner over the entire area, then wipe clean, using your squeegee if you have one. If grout has become discolored or dirty, use a grout cleaner and a scrub brush, or try straight baking soda.

If your bathtub is acrylic or fiberglass, spray with an all-purpose cleaner or a tub and tile cleaner and wipe with a sponge, scrubbing if necessary. Don't use an abrasive

cleanser on these tubs. If your tub is enameled steel, you can use a stronger cleanser and a scrub brush, or a nontoxic scouring powder such as Bon Ami. If your shower stall is plastic, use an all-purpose cleaner and your squeegee. If the shower door is glass, use a glass cleaner. You can also try a spray of straight distilled white vinegar; let it sit for ten minutes, then wipe or squeegee off.

Avoid chemically based shower and tub products meant to be sprayed after every bath. These products will significantly increase your family's chemical exposure. If you want to address potential buildup on a daily basis, try spraying a solution of half water and half distilled white vinegar, or a store-bought nontoxic spray.

Other Bathroom Tasks

Sink

Wiping the sink with a sponge after every use will prevent soap scum and lime or mineral deposits from building up. Clean bathroom sinks and counters with an all-purpose bathroom cleaner. Avoid abrasives on porcelain. Use a toothbrush and a strong natural cleaner to scrub grime that builds up around faucets — or try using straight salt. Rinse well. Don't forget to wash your toothbrush holder. To make chrome fixtures really shine, try a nontoxic glass cleaner (see Product Guide, page 165).

Drips

Don't ignore a dripping faucet or a toilet that won't stop running — these can waste a lot of water. Simple fixes for these problems can often be found in a basic home how-to book. For mineral stains from faucet drips, try rubbing the area with salt and distilled white vinegar.

Floors

Most bathroom floors can be damp mopped (after sweeping) with an all-purpose floor cleaner, or you may choose to use one formulated for your floor type. (See page 63 for more tips on cleaning floors.) Never use a soap-based cleanser on stone floors as it can make the surface extremely slippery, and don't use detergents on marble, as they can eat away and/or dull the surface. For stains on marble, try flushing them with cold water, then gently scrubbing with your pumice stone.

Consider placing a small recycling bin in the bathroom if you have the space; many containers for soaps, shampoos, and cosmetics can be recycled. Check the packaging and your local regulations.

5 : AROUND THE HOUSE

THE MAJOR LIVING SPACES OF OUR
HOMES — DINING ROOM, LIVING ROOM,
AND BEDROOM — ARE THE ONES THAT
MOST REFLECT OUR FAMILIES' LIFESTYLE,
WHETHER WE CHOOSE TO RELAX IN A
COZY ARMCHAIR OR TO SERVE A
FORMAL DINNER WITH FINE CHINA. OUR
BEDROOMS ARE OUR SANCTUARIES,
WHERE WE RECHARGE AFTER HECTIC

DAYS. MANY OF US HAVE HOME OFFICES, WHERE WE MANAGE THE HOUSEHOLD OR EVEN RUN A BUSINESS. CHILDREN'S ROOMS FUNCTION AS PLAY SPACES AS WELL AS PLACES TO NAP AND SLEEP.

A cleaning strategy for these rooms ought to preserve as much time as possible for actually using them, while providing for a healthy indoor environment. As with any part of the house, moving away from chemical cleaners will reduce your family's exposure to toxins. Indoor air quality may be the most important issue around the house — be especially vigilant about using nontoxic carpet cleaners and other products that will stick around. Using green products and practices will allow you to clean your home efficiently and safely, leaving you free to read, to entertain, to work — to live.

Getting Started

Cleaning tasks are less intense outside the kitchen, bathroom, and laundry room. Keeping the rest of the house clean usually comes down to three steps: declutter, dust, and vacuum.

Decluttering opens up your living spaces visually and means there will be fewer surfaces that can collect dust. These rooms also have a tendency to pile up with stuff as people use them and pass through them. Encourage your family members to pick up after themselves daily.

Dust is not just an aesthetic nuisance — it's a health issue, too. What we call dust is a combination of dirt, mites, dead skin, and other particles. Chemicals including lead and PCBs are routinely found in household dust. Excessive dust can irritate respiratory systems, inflame allergies, and encourage the growth of mold spores. Dust and dust mites are also potent asthma triggers. If you or a family member has allergies, invest in a HEPA-filtered vacuum.

The best tools for dusting are a vacuum, some soft cloths or rags, and a plant-based cleaning product. Many of us are tempted to use oily products and sprays to wipe up dust, in hopes that they will moisturize and leave a sheen. However, the residue they leave will actually attract more dust.

After dusting, vacuum rugs and carpets. For a more thorough cleaning, move the furniture to the center of the room and clean corners, baseboards, and walls. If a lot of dirt gets tracked in, or if you have pets, it may be necessary to dust and vacuum more often.

Around the House Checklist

DAILY

- [ ] Straighten and pick up clutter.
- [ ] Make beds.
- [ ] Sweep or vacuum as necessary.
- [ ] Deal with stains.

WEEKLY

- [ ] Dust.
- [ ] Damp mop floors.
- [ ] Change bed linens.
- [ ] Empty hampers and do laundry.
- [ ] Vacuum upholstered furniture and drapes.
- [ ] Sweep the garage or basement if they are used regularly.

MONTHLY

- [ ] Turn mattresses.
- [ ] Wash or air out pillows.
- [ ] Vacuum underneath and behind furniture.
- [ ] Wash windows as necessary.
- [ ] Clean furnace filters if furnace is in use.
- [ ] Check the seals on toxic items in storage.
- [ ] Vacuum or sweep spaces that aren't in regular use.

BIANNUALLY

- [ ] Air out mattresses.
- [ ] Clean drapes and curtains.
- [ ] Wash rugs.

Indoor Air Quality

The air inside our homes can be two to five times more polluted than the air outside. Common sources of indoor air pollution are volatile organic compounds (VOCs) from cleaning products, pesticides, and other everyday household products, as well as outgassing from carpets, furniture, and other chemically treated materials. The chemicals and other substances that hang around in the air of many homes cause or exacerbate a wide range of maladies, from respiratory congestion and asthma to headaches and nausea.

Eliminating toxic products and pesticides from your home and adopting green cleaning practices will improve indoor air quality. Make sure your home is well ventilated; airtight homes can produce "sick building syndrome" (see page 15). Avoid furniture made from particleboard or other composites; they frequently emit trace amounts of formaldehyde. If you're doing any home improvement, choose low-VOC paint, insulation, and other products.

Indoor plants can dramatically improve air quality. All plants convert carbon dioxide to oxygen, but some actually remove chemicals like

A good source for information about indoor air quality is the EPA's "The Inside Story: A Guide to Indoor Air Quality," available at *www.epa.gov/iaq.*

Chlorphytum
(Spider plant)

Aglaonema
(Chinese Evergreen)

Spathiphyllum
(Peacelily)

Syngonium
(Arrowhead Vine)

Hedera
(English Ivy)

Dracaena
(Cornplant)

Scindapsus
(Devil's Ivy)

benzene and formaldehyde from the air. The most effective air cleaners are Aglaonema (Chinese evergreen), Spathiphyllum (peacelily), Syngonium (arrowhead vine), Hedera (English ivy), Dracaena (cornplant), spider plants, and Scindapsus (devil's ivy). Daisies and chrysanthemums are good, too. Aim for roughly 15 plants for every 1,500 square feet in your house. Remember that your plants need to breathe, too — dust them gently with a damp cloth. Keep their soil or root area clear — some of the air-cleaning action occurs there.

Conventional air fresheners — sprays, containers, and plug-ins — are potent chemical cocktails. If you are concerned about odors in your home, try boiling some water with a few cloves in it, or putting a few drops of essential oil on a working lightbulb. For more on air fresheners, see pages 76–77.

Caring for Furniture

Wood Furniture

Most modern wood furniture doesn't need to be waxed or polished. It was likely given a finish at the factory that wax won't even penetrate. Wipe wood surfaces clean with a soft cloth; if you do want the sheen of polished furniture, use an ecofriendly cleaner (see Product Guide, page 169) or try one of the polishes in the Recipes chapter (page 141). Bamboo and rattan require only dusting. Avoid traditional furniture cleaners and polishes — they often contain ammonia and formaldehyde.

Upholstered Furniture

Vacuum upholstered furniture weekly to remove dust. If there is an odor problem, try sprinkling baking soda before vacuuming. Don't use commercial fabric "fresheners" — these usually contain fragrances or solvents that can irritate nasal passages, eyes, or lungs and may be harmful to the environment. Nontoxic stain removers (see page 163) can take care of many stains; some nontoxic carpet cleaners, such as Capture (see page 90), are also effective on upholstery. The Stain Guide details remedies for many specific upholstery stains.

Some upholstered furniture can be treated to repel stains. Traditional stain protectors such as Scotchgard are not green products; instead, look for a silicone-based treatment; it is an inert natural substance that will repel most spills, although it is not effective against grease.

Leather Furniture

Leather furniture should be vacuumed regularly. Most leather furniture has a finish that will prevent stains and spots. For scuff marks, try a pencil eraser; for water marks, try rubbing with distilled white vinegar. (Always test any stain treatment on an inconspicuous spot.) There are few natural leather cleaners available; try the simple leather polish in the Recipes chapter (page 144). If you do use a chemically based one, be sure to air out the room afterward.

Cleaning Windows and Drapes

Most window cleaners contain ammonia, a substance to be avoided; it is highly irritating to the eyes and lungs. Use a nontoxic, ammonia-free window cleaner instead, or try one of the recipes on page 145. Wipe with a clean soft cloth or a squeegee. Don't use newspaper — it usually gets ink on your hands and on the window frame.

Vacuum drapes with a brush attachment, and launder them every six months or so. Sheers and light panels can usually go in the washing machine — check the manufacturer's directions. If you must take your drapes to a dry cleaner, choose one that uses environmentally friendly or "wet" methods. You can also wash curtains in your machine and hang them to dry; a dry cleaner can do the pressing if necessary.

Lamps

Many lamp shades can be vacuumed using a drapery attachment. A lint roller also makes a good shade-dusting tool. Cleaning the base depends on its material: an all-purpose cleaner will work on many surfaces. Feather dusters are excellent for use on chandeliers — the oil in the feathers picks up the dust. To really clean a chandelier, take it down, then take it apart and clean each element separately, though this time-consuming task can be done yearly or even less often.

Caring for Books

Sunlight is the greatest enemy of paper — try to position your bookshelves out of direct sunlight. Dust shelved books once a month or as necessary. You can also vacuum shelved books (use a brush attachment), though take care with precious volumes.

Carpets and Rugs

A clean carpet makes the whole room feel brighter and cleaner. Over time, though, spills and marks are inevitable. Deal with stains as they happen. See the Stain Guide for specific treatments, but always follow this basic rule of thumb: Never scrub, and instead always blot with a clean, soft towel. Scrubbing will just push the stain deeper into the pile. Vacuum your carpet and rugs regularly; accumulated dirt can be ground into the pile, reducing its lifespan.

There are a number of nontoxic carpet cleaners on the market; see the following page and the Product Guide, page 163. These products are safer than traditional carpet cleaners, which may contain perchlorethylene, a chemical that can affect the central nervous system, and naphthalene, which is extremely toxic to children. Naphthalene is also known to accumulate in marine life.

It's particularly important to use a nontoxic carpet treatment, since the cleaning product may persist in your home, getting kicked up into the air under normal wear and with every vacuum. Carpet-cleaning products that contain chlorine, fragrance, and other chemicals can be harmful to your family's health.

Sprinkle onto carpet and stains.

Powder absorbs stains and dirt.

Removes household allergens.

A good choice is a powder called Capture, which is nontoxic and which helps to remove household allergens. (The product's effectiveness was verified in a 1996 study by Johns Hopkins University and Air Quality Sciences.)

The slightly damp powder contains a water-based cleanser; after it's sprinkled on a carpet, the powder absorbs oily and water-based stains and dirt. (Vacuuming alone is not very effective on these kinds of stains.) After the powder sits for a half-hour, vacuum it up. It is effective on smaller soiled portions and for cleaning an entire room.

For cleaning hardwood, tile, and other uncarpeted floors, see the Kitchen chapter, page 63.

Bedroom

It's especially important to keep bedrooms as dust- and irritant-free as possible in order to reduce allergens. Choose natural fibers for bed linens — they make it easier for skin to breathe, thus enhancing the detoxification that naturally occurs during sleep. Look for organic cotton — most other cotton is the product of large-scale, chemically intensive farming processes. Also avoid polyester and polyester blends, which may have been sprayed with formaldehyde to prevent wrinkles. Synthetics also tend to require fabric softener, which often contains harsh or harmful chemicals.

Mattress

Vacuum the mattress when you change the bed linens each week. It's the easiest way to remove dust, mites, dead skin, and other particles. Air the mattress out twice a year. Ideally, bring the mattresses outdoors for a few hours — the ultraviolet rays in sunlight are a natural disinfectant. If outdoor airing isn't practical, try putting the mattress in the middle of an empty room with the windows open.

Pillows

Wash pillows every few months in the bathtub, using some liquid laundry detergent. Let them air dry thoroughly. Down pillows can go in automatic washers on the gentle cycle — add a clean sneaker or two to prevent bunching. Never put foam pillows in the washer or dryer; wash them by hand and let them air dry.

Blankets

Wash blankets separately, one per load, every six months or so. Down comforters can usually be treated the same as down pillows, but check the manufacturer's washing instructions first.

Closets

Closets can become musty and vulnerable to mold and mildew if they're not well ventilated. Leave the closet doors open occasionally to air things out. To deodorize, place an open box of baking soda in a spot where it won't get knocked over, or try filling an old sock with clay kitty litter. Twice a year, clean out the entire closet.

Moth balls contain naphthalene, a neurotoxin and respiratory irritant. An excellent alternative moth repellent is cedar — in the form of a spray, an oil, or wood blocks and hangers. Sand blocks every month or two to expose new wood and oil. A sachet filled with lavender and/or cedar chips is another good solution.

Baby's Room

Young, developing bodies can be especially vulnerable to chemical exposure. Keeping a child's room free of harmful substances achieves one of the principal goals of green cleaning: to create a healthy environment for future generations.

If you are already making a habit of using plant-based and other nontoxic products in your cleaning practice, you probably don't need to purchase any special items for cleaning and maintaining your child's room. Be sure that any product you use is fragrance- and chlorine-free.

Kids' metabolisms, their ability to process toxins, and their eating habits are all different than adults'. In many cases, this makes children more susceptible to chemical harm (though in some cases, those differences can actually protect kids.) The basic rule of thumb is: better safe than sorry. Even low-level exposure to toxins can cause changes to reproductive and immune systems and the brain.

Of course, children go hand in hand with spills and stains. You may wish to clean this room more often, and to pay special attention to surfaces small hands and mouths come into contact with.

Wipe the changing area after every diaper change with a natural cleaner; enzyme-based cleansers are especially effective on organic materials. For specific stains, see the Stain Guide.

☠ If you are painting the nursery or redecorating a child's room, use one of the new breed of nontoxic, low-VOC paints.

Diapers

The cloth-versus-disposable question is a challenging one for many families. The most environmentally sound choice is to use cloth diapers and to launder them at home. However, that isn't always possible. If you choose to use disposable diapers, look for ones that are chlorine-free and fragrance-free. No matter which diapers you are using, flush waste down the toilet rather than throwing it away; it is not good for landfills.

If you're using cloth, rinse diapers in the toilet after dumping waste, then put them in your diaper pail. (Make sure that your pail has a tight-fitting lid.) Soak the diapers in the pail with a solution that's one part distilled white vinegar to ten parts water. About two dozen diapers make one laundry load.

If your baby is drinking formula, it can be difficult to keep up with bottle washing. Try to get in the habit of rinsing each bottle with cold water as soon as it is emptied — this will make it easier to wash when you do get around to it.

Pets

Shampoos

There are several types of natural, nontoxic pet shampoos available; some are formulated to reduce dander, which is a major allergen for humans. Brush your pets regularly — this is enjoyable for them, good for their coats, and will reduce the amount of animal hair around your house. Sprinkling a bit of baking soda on your pet before brushing can help control odor.

Fleas

There are some natural options to help keep fleas away from your pets if they go outside. Adding orange oil to your pet's shampoo and washing your pet frequently are helpful — you can also try adding brewer's yeast to your pet's food. If you must use a chemical-based repellent, try one of the longer-term products that require application only every few weeks. If your pet does get fleas, try a flea comb before using a flea shampoo. Vacuum bedding and sleeping areas thoroughly and dispose of the vacuum bag immediately — continue this for several weeks, as the fleas may have laid eggs.

Kitty Litter

Cat owners should choose a biodegradable, fragrance-free kitty litter. Lining the litter box with newspaper and sprinkling it with baking soda will keep it fresh-smelling longer. If your cat tends to kick litter outside the box, consider a domed model. Sift the litter daily and dispose of waste. Change it weekly (more frequently if you have more than one pet), and clean the box itself with an all-purpose cleaner.

Your pet had a run-in with a skunk? The oldest way to deal with the problem is still the best way: tomato juice. Buy the largest container you can find and soak your pet thoroughly, for as long as possible; then rinse.

The Home Office

Whether your home office is used for a small business or for household management, it is essential that it be organized and clean. Take care to arrange your office in an ergonomically sound way, in order to protect against injury. Use space efficiently — try using walls for vertical storage, with a peg-and-board or hanging file system.

Dust

Computers, printers, and other electronics rapidly accumulate dust. Keeping a small feather duster in an accessible place is a good way to make sure that you dust frequently. Clean them with a mild all-purpose formula — spritz it onto a cloth and wipe; never spray directly onto the item. Computer screens require special attention. Use a window cleaner that doesn't contain ammonia or alcohol (see Recipes, page 145, and the Product Guide, page 166), or use an anti-static cloth. Your keyboard will collect dust and bits of debris; use your vacuum (set on low) with a brush attachment to get material out from between keys.

Green cleaning is great for your workplace's health, too. Share cleaning and recycling ideas with your coworkers, and with your facilities manager.

Reduce Waste

The biggest waste problem in a home office is paper. Print only when you need to, and conscientiously recycle your paper. Be sure to turn equipment off when not in use. See page 180 for information on handling obsolete equipment. Even nonworking items can be recycled or reused.

Attic

The main problems you'll face in the attic are dust, lack of ventilation, and pests. If the space has been neglected for some time, you may wish to rent a shop vac to thoroughly remove dust and cobwebs. If the floor is unfinished wood, consider sealing it — it will speed up sweeping or vacuuming. Use a nontoxic sealant; a variety are available through online stores such as Green Home *(www.greenhome.com)*.

Your attic should be properly ventilated to aid cooling in summer months. A ceiling fan may seem like an extravagance, but it can make a big difference in moving hot air out and cooler air in. Make sure the attic has a smoke detector and check it regularly.

Storing a small vacuum cleaner in the attic will save you from having to lug a heavy model up the stairs.

There are natural ways to protect items in storage. Balls of cotton soaked with lavender or eucalyptus essential oils will help ward off moths, while muslin bags filled with baking soda or charcoal can protect against humidity and odors. You can also scatter dried citrus peels and whole cloves among clothing before storing it for the summer.

Basement

If your basement floor is unsealed concrete, consider sealing it. It will be easier to sweep or vacuum. Look for a silicone-based or other nontoxic sealant. Another type of green sealant is waterglass, or sodium silicate, which can also be used on walls to inhibit mildew. Vacuum or sweep a concrete floor regularly and damp mop monthly, depending on the traffic in your basement.

The basement is a common entryway for pests. Be certain that any holes or crevices are sealed. Be disciplined about clutter. Cull your stored material annually and dispose of unwanted items by recycling them, donating them to charity, or selling them at a yard sale.

If your basement has a furnace, be sure to keep the filters clean. Clean them once before winter begins, and then monthly while the furnace is in use. A clean filter will prevent dust from circulating throughout the house and will help the furnace work more efficiently. Most filters can be washed with mild laundry detergent; check the instructions for your furnace. Have a professional check the unit's motor and fan once a year, the ductwork and vents every few years. If you have a gas furnace, be sure to install a carbon monoxide detector in your home and check its batteries every other month.

Unwanted moisture is always a concern in the basement, as it fosters the growth of mold and mildew. Don't leave a liquid spill to dry naturally — mop it up immediately. Wiping down walls and floors with distilled white vinegar every few months can help prevent mold from growing. See page 71 for more tips on dealing with mold and mildew.

If your basement smells musty, leave out a tray of clay kitty litter or several open boxes of baking soda.

Garage

If you garage your car, be vigilant about fumes. Never run the car with the garage door closed, and be sure to install a carbon monoxide detector in the garage.

If your garage has an unsealed concrete floor, consider sealing it with a safe, nontoxic sealant (see Basement, opposite). Prevent oil spills and stains by keeping a drip tray or several layers of cardboard beneath your car. If an oil spill does occur, promptly pour some clay kitty litter mixed with baking soda onto the spill and grind it in with your foot. Let it sit for a while, then sweep it up. If a spot remains, try a paste of baking soda and water. If a spill has already dried by the time you find it, wet the stain before applying the kitty litter mixture.

The garage is often where the most toxic household items — motor oil, batteries, paint, brake fluid — are stored. See the Storage, Disposal & Recycling chapter for information on how to safely store and dispose of these products. If you have children in your home, keep these dangerous substances locked up. Check the seals on all toxic items regularly.

Animals are often attracted to conventional antifreeze, which has a sweet taste but is a deadly poison. Switch to a safer formulation made with propylene glycol, such as the brand Sierra. Clean up spills immediately.

6 : LAUNDRY

A GREEN APPROACH TO LAUNDRY OFFERS
SIGNIFICANT REWARDS. REDUCING THE
NUMBER OF CHEMICALS AND TOXINS
THAT COME INTO CONTACT WITH LOVED
ONES AS THEY EAT, PLAY, AND SLEEP
IS AN IMMEDIATE BENEFIT, BUT GREEN
CLEANING ALSO PROTECTS LOCAL
WATER SUPPLIES AND CAN REDUCE
ENERGY COSTS. LAUNDRY PRODUCTS

ARE AMONG THE HARSHEST HOUSEHOLD CHEMICALS — ELIMINATING THEM FROM OUR CLEANING PRACTICE IS ESSENTIAL.

Freshly laundered clothing and bedding is a sensual experience like no other. Often when we wash our family's clothes, we are minding their memories—a lucky dress or a favorite shirt must be cared for properly and returned to its owner in the best possible condition. Doing this task with a green mind-set protects both those memories and the future.

Getting Started

The simplest, most immediate way to detoxify our laundry is to stop using traditional laundry detergents, bleaches, softeners, and other additives. Many commercially available laundry detergents are petroleum-based, which means they deplete a nonrenewable resource, create pollution during their manufacture, and burden wastewater. Chemically derived formulas may also use synthetic surfactants, substances that break down into a compound known to mimic estrogen. (Plant-based or biodegradable surfactants do not contribute to this problem.) Chlorine bleach is another substance to avoid. It is caustic, poisonous, and highly reactive, readily combining with other chemicals to form noxious compounds.

There are green alternatives available to replace these products. Many supermarkets and specialty stores now stock a variety of plant-based, phosphate-free laundry soaps and detergents, as well as chlorine-free bleach. See the Product Guide (pages 162–63) for the best products and tips on where to buy them, or try the simple, do-it-yourself laundry soap, bleach, and starch in Recipes, page 142.

Male Pregnancy?

Estrogen-mimicking chemicals, including those found in or created by laundry products, can block the action of male hormones, altering how male animals develop. Such chemicals were blamed for a 2004 outbreak of egg-bearing male fish in the Potomac River.

Laundry Basics

Take a moment and consider the way clothing travels through your home. At each stopping point, the proper tools should be available. The process of doing laundry offers many opportunities to substitute environmentally friendly products and practices for older and possibly toxic ones. By looking at the whole system, it's easier to identify simple but effective changes to make.

Hampers

Place a hamper in every room where people change clothes — not just bedrooms and bathrooms, but also places like mudrooms, where wet swimsuits or mittens are shed. Sturdy cotton hamper liners can be used for easier transport, though they will require washing from time to time. Wipe plastic hampers with a mix of distilled white vinegar and water weekly; sprinkle baking soda in the bottom of every type of hamper to absorb odors.

Sorting

Once you've hauled your clothes and linens to the laundry room, properly sorting them saves time and makes for cleaner clothing. Always check the label on any item of clothing you aren't sure about (see page 106). While you're sorting, take the time to look for stains and treat them. (See the Stain Guide.) Remove any items that must be dry-cleaned or hand-washed and put them in bins or laundry bags you've reserved for this purpose. Then, organize clothes into loads according to these categories:

- Machine-washable delicates
- Colored bed linens and towels
- White bed linens and towels
- Thin white clothing
- Heavy white clothing
- Slightly soiled colored clothing
- Slightly soiled dark clothing

◎ Very soiled colored clothing

◎ Very soiled dark clothing

Put delicates into a lingerie bag or a pillowcase — they can then be washed along with similarly colored items. Other things to do while sorting: empty pockets, turn jeans and corduroy items inside out, close zippers, and tie drawstrings so they won't be lost. If a zipper is sticking, run a bar of soap or a candle along it, then try again.

Laundry Checklist

DAILY

- [ ] Treat stains as they happen.
- [ ] Put dirty clothes in hampers.

WEEKLY

- [ ] Change sheets and towels.
- [ ] Sort clothes and pretreat stains.
- [ ] Run washing machine.
- [ ] Dry clothing and bedding.
- [ ] Fold and iron.

BIMONTHLY

- [ ] Hand wash delicates and deal with "dry clean only" items.

MONTHLY

- [ ] Air out bedding and wash as necessary.
- [ ] Wash kitchen and bathroom rugs.

Guide to Laundry Labels

Always pay attention to fabric care labels — proper laundering will help your clothes last longer and come out cleaner.

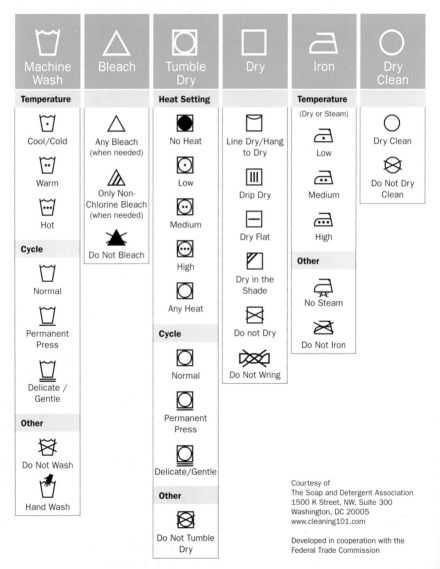

Machine Wash	Bleach	Tumble Dry	Dry	Iron	Dry Clean

Machine Wash — Temperature
- Cool/Cold
- Warm
- Hot

Machine Wash — Cycle
- Normal
- Permanent Press
- Delicate / Gentle

Machine Wash — Other
- Do Not Wash
- Hand Wash

Bleach
- Any Bleach (when needed)
- Only Non-Chlorine Bleach (when needed)
- Do Not Bleach

Tumble Dry — Heat Setting
- No Heat
- Low
- Medium
- High
- Any Heat

Tumble Dry — Cycle
- Normal
- Permanent Press
- Delicate/Gentle

Tumble Dry — Other
- Do Not Tumble Dry

Dry
- Line Dry/Hang to Dry
- Drip Dry
- Dry Flat
- Dry in the Shade
- Do not Dry
- Do Not Wring

Iron — Temperature (Dry or Steam)
- Low
- Medium
- High

Iron — Other
- No Steam
- Do Not Iron

Dry Clean
- Dry Clean
- Do Not Dry Clean

Courtesy of
The Soap and Detergent Association
1500 K Street, NW, Suite 300
Washington, DC 20005
www.cleaning101.com

Developed in cooperation with the
Federal Trade Commission

Doing the Wash

Use a plant-based, fragrance-free laundry soap or detergent, or make your own with one of the recipes from the Recipes chapter. If you are using store-bought detergent, you probably don't need as much as the manufacturer recommends — try using one-third to one-half less, even with the ecofriendly brands.

Water Temperature

Choose water temperature based on the type of fabric and amount of soil in each load. Generally, hot water is only necessary for whites; everything else can be washed in warm or cold water. (More than 85 percent of the energy used by the average washer goes to heating water.) Use a cold rinse cycle for every load.

☀ Fels-Naptha soap, which many people swear by for laundry, does not contain naphthalene, a potentially dangerous chemical.

To save both water and energy, always choose the shortest cycle and wash time possible. Don't overload the washer, or clothes won't get clean. Some simple additives can improve your wash: a quarter cup of baking soda works as a fabric softener; to reduce static cling, add a quarter cup of distilled white vinegar. In either case, add during the wash cycle if you are using liquid laundry detergent, and during the rinse cycle if you are using a powder.

Treating Stains

Ideally, stains should be treated immediately, before clothing goes into the hamper or laundry basket. Time is of the essence; a fresh stain can be easy to treat, while one that has set overnight or longer may be impossible to remove. It's important to identify stains properly in order to treat them — see the Stain Guide for more information and for specific stain-removal recipes.

Test fabrics for colorfastness before attempting any stain removal. To do this, snip a scrap of fabric from the inside of a seam and place it in a shallow bowl with a small amount of the stain remover for about ten minutes. Rinse, then compare the scrap with the untreated fabric.

Once a year, put a cup or more of distilled white vinegar in the washing machine and run a full cycle to clean it.

Hand Washing Delicates

Hand washing is time consuming, and it uses a great deal of water for only a few items. Reserve hand washing for delicate items that don't get very dirty and may be damaged from the agitation of an automatic washer.

Use two basins, the first filled with warm soapy water. Use a nontoxic liquid laundry detergent or the basic laundry detergent recipe on page 142. Fill the second basin with room temperature water — you can add a bit of distilled white vinegar to brighten colors or whites. (As with washing machines, keep dark and light colors separate; any garment that will bleed color should get its own basin.) Swish each item through the soapy water for a few minutes, then rinse and press it against the edge of the basin to squeeze water out. (These are delicates — don't wring them.) You can further dry the item by pressing with a clean towel. Then let it air dry on a rack.

Drying

Old-fashioned air drying obviously uses less energy than automatic clothes dryers, and it leaves clothes smelling especially fresh. The best kind of air drying happens outdoors, with fresh air and sunshine. For indoor drying, there are a variety of space-saving clotheslines and racks available. If you are using an automatic dryer, make the task as energy-efficient as possible. Clean

Swish

Rinse and press against bowl edge

Press with towel

the lint filter between every load, and don't overdry. Avoid chemical fabric softener sheets, which coat clothes with wax and perfumes, can cause skin irritation, and may contain several different dangerous chemicals. The best time to use fabric softener is in the washing machine; some nontoxic laundry detergents include a fabric softener. If you'd like to add fragrance in the dryer, put a few drops of essential oil on a cotton cloth, then place it in with the wet clothes.

Folding and Ironing

Fold clothes as soon as they are dry in order to prevent wrinkling. Items that require ironing can be hung up and put aside until the folding is done. If there is residue on the iron, or it begins to stick, sprinkle some salt on a piece of paper and run the iron over it until it runs smoothly again. Between uses, clean the iron with a paste of baking soda and water, then wipe clean with a soft cloth — never use abrasives.

Commercially available spray starches often contain formaldehyde and other irritants. You can make your own clothing starch by putting two tablespoons of cornstarch in a spray bottle full of water.

☼ To fight static cling without chemically based dryer sheets, try drying cottons and synthetics separately.

Dry Cleaning Alternatives

Commercial dry cleaning is a toxic process. "Dry cleaning" usually means running clothing through a chemical solution. Most dry cleaners use a petroleum-based solvent called perchlorethylene, which can adversely affect the central nervous system; can irritate the skin, eyes, nose, and throat; and is a possible human carcinogen. Perc, as it's frequently called, has become one of the most common contaminants in groundwater.

There are alternatives to standard dry cleaning. Some commercial dry cleaners offer "wet cleaning," which depends on computer-controlled washers and nontoxic detergents. Another non-perc process uses liquid carbon dioxide. Both avoid the noxious smell of perc-cleaned clothes, as well as the environmental hazards of the chemical.

Many items labeled "dry clean only" can be successfully laundered at home using simple, nontoxic solutions. Avoid home dry cleaning kits, which are perc-free but often contain detergents, perfumes, and chemical emulsifiers. To clean "dry clean only" items at home, base your method on the fiber content of the clothing — see opposite. Use the hand washing method outlined on the previous page.

Special Fabrics

Acetate and Rayon

Gently hand wash with mild laundry detergent (i.e., free of chlorine bleaches or harsh chemicals) in cool water. Don't use acidic rinses such as vinegar on rayon. Always be gentle with these fabrics — they can easily abrade. Line-dry or lay flat.

Cashmere and Wool

Gently hand wash with mild, low-pH laundry detergent in cool water. If the fabric has a soapy residue, rinse it in distilled white vinegar. Block each item — that is, stretch it gently in order to restore it to its original size — and let it dry flat on a sweater rack.

Silk

Hand wash silk in warm water using a very gentle laundry detergent. Do not use washing soda– or baking soda–based soaps; they can damage the material. If you have hard water, add a tablespoon or two of distilled white vinegar to the rinsewater. Line dry indoors.

Leather and Suede

Most leather garments are "finished," which means they have a protective coating. You can generally wipe off spills with a damp cloth. Unfortunately, to effectively clean an entire leather or suede garment requires the services of a professional leather cleaner, who will usually use chemically based methods. Ask your local cleaner what types of solvents are used and if they offer perc-free alternatives. To clean spots and stains from suede, try a suede brush, another piece of suede, or very fine sandpaper. (Test it on a hidden area of the garment first.)

☠ If you do use a traditional dry cleaner, immediately remove any plastic wrapping and air out clothes thoroughly before wearing or storing.

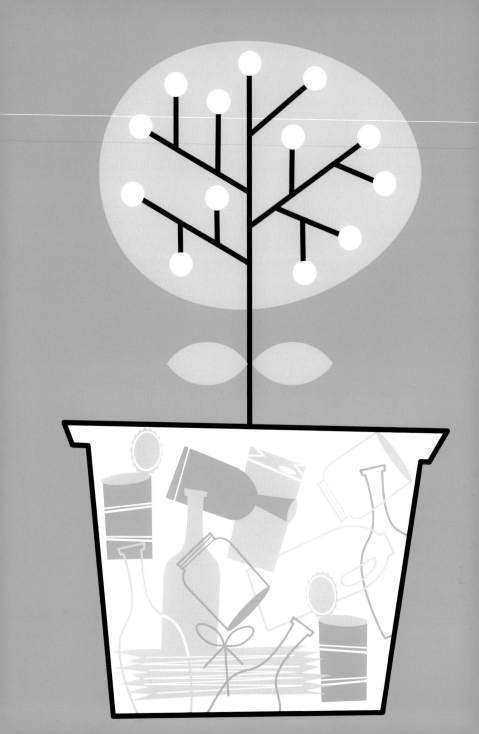

7 : STORAGE, DISPOSAL & RECYCLING

THE AVERAGE AMERICAN HOME HAS
SOME HUNDRED POUNDS OF HAZARDOUS
HOUSEHOLD PRODUCTS STORED IN ITS
BASEMENT, GARAGE, STORAGE SHED,
AND CLOSETS. CHANCES ARE YOUR
HOUSE IS NO EXCEPTION. AS YOU CLEAN
AND DECLUTTER YOUR SURROUNDINGS,
YOU'LL HAVE QUESTIONS ABOUT HOW TO

STORE THE HAZARDOUS PRODUCTS YOU FEEL YOU NEED TO KEEP, AND ABOUT HOW TO DISPOSE OF THOSE YOU KNOW YOU DON'T WANT UNDER YOUR ROOF. THIS CHAPTER GIVES YOU TIPS ON SAFE STORAGE AND THE BEST METHODS FOR DISPOSAL. YOU'LL FIND OUT WHAT PRODUCTS ARE THE WORST ENVIRONMENTAL OFFENDERS, AND YOU'LL LEARN THE BEST WAY TO ORGANIZE AND STORE YOUR CLEANING SUPPLIES.

A green home is a home that recycles. Bottles, cans, and newspapers are easy to handle — take them to the curb or the supermarket. But what about carpet, computers, cell phones, and food scraps? Almost everything is recyclable — and if it's not, it may be a perfect nutrient for a compost pile.

First Things First

The first line of defense against hazardous household waste is to avoid using harmful chemicals in the first place. Instead of accumulating more and more dangerous products, think before you buy. Look for safer alternatives. Buy the least hazardous product.

Most Common Hazardous Products Around the House

Automotive products: Gasoline, motor oil, antifreeze, windshield wiper fluid, car wax and cleaners, lead-acid batteries, brake fluid, transmission fluid

Home improvement products: Paint, varnish, stain, paint thinner, paint stripper, caulk, adhesives

Household cleaners: drain opener, oven cleaner, tub and tile cleaner, toilet bowl cleaner, spot remover, bleach, ammonia, furniture polish and wax

Other products: Batteries, nail polish, pool chemicals, shoe polish, lighter fluid, prescription medicines, some arts and crafts materials, some personal care products

Pesticides: Insecticide and insect repellent, weed killer, rat and mouse poison, pet spray and dip, flea collars, moth balls, disinfectant, wood preservative

It's difficult to be a homeowner without using any hazardous products. If you must purchase a product containing toxic chemicals, buy only as much as you need to do the job at hand, then store or dispose of the material properly.

Learn how to read labels. Federal law requires that hazardous products include clearly visible signal words on their labels, along with the name of the hazardous substance and a description of the hazard (such as "causes burns" or "toxic if absorbed through the skin"). The words "danger" or "poison" indicate a highly toxic, corrosive, or extremely flammable product that can cause serious injury or even death if misused or ingested. "Warning" or "caution" indicate a moderately or slightly toxic product — that is, one unlikely to cause permanent injury if first aid is given. "Nontoxic" is a marketing term and doesn't necessarily mean the product is entirely free of hazardous ingredients. Read the entire label for health warnings and use good judgment. Look for products that are biodegradable and contain natural ingredients.

Proper Storage

Store hazardous products in as few places as possible, keeping items of like kind, purpose, and safety level together to reduce the risk of mistaking one thing for another. The best location is outside the house, in a garage or shed. Keep all hazardous products away from heat, flame, or sparks. Try to keep very hazardous substances together, and keep them apart from relatively safe ones. Do not store pesticides in a food cabinet, for example, or dog food next to charcoal briquettes.

If there are children or pets in the home, store dangerous products on high shelves, in locked cabinets, or in cabinets with childproof latches. Storage places should be cool (but above freezing), dry, and away from foodstuffs.

The bathroom medicine cabinet makes a great first project. Keep medicines in their original containers and store them on the top shelf, where small children can't see them. If any container or bottle lacks a label, throw it away. Remember to put a lock or childproof latch on the door if you have kids. Never store medicines with food, cleaning supplies, or other household substances.

Healthy Home Tips

- Store products in their original containers with labels intact and legible. Never deviate from this rule!

- Never put dangerous substances in unlabeled bottles or containers.

- Any product with the words "poison," "danger," "warning," or "caution" on the label belongs in a childproof cabinet.

- Childproof all medicine cabinets, hobby and workshop storage cabinets, and cleaning supply cupboards.

- Store outdoor pesticides outside the house, with gardening and lawn supplies.

- Never reuse pesticide containers or the containers of any other toxic substances for any purpose.

- Do not mix products unless the label specifically instructs you to do so. Mixing products can cause explosive or poisonous chemical reactions. Different brands of the same product may contain incompatible ingredients.

- Even empty containers can pose hazards.

Corrosives

Keep corrosive products — drain cleaner, oven cleaner, lye, etc. — together. If a container begins to corrode, place the entire container in a plastic bucket or glass jar with a tight-fitting lid. Pack nonflammable absorbent materials, such as clay-based kitty litter or vermiculite, around it. Clearly label the outside container to indicate contents and appropriate warnings, then dispose of it appropriately (see pages 122–23).

Flammables

Exercise caution with flammable products such as gasoline and motor oil. These materials should be stored in approved containers outside the house, in a well-ventilated garage or storage shed, away from all sources of heat, flame, sparks, or other sources of ignition such as pilot lights, electrical switches, and motors. Keep a dry-chemical or sodium bicarbonate fire extinguisher near where you store flammable supplies, and install a non-ionizing smoke detector nearby. The best disposal method for these products is to use them up.

- Aerosols are flammable products. Store away from all sources of heat, flame, or sparks.

- Storage is not an option for rags contaminated with paint stripper or remover, wood stain, gasoline, or other petroleum

products; they can spontane-
ously combust if left to sit for
too long. If immediate disposal
isn't possible and if there are no
directions for rag disposal on
the product label, place them
in an airtight metal container
and store the container outside
the house and away from other
structures until it can be picked
up with the trash.

● Store liquid propane gas tanks
outdoors, away from all sources
of heat, flame, or sparks.

☠ The American Associa-
tion of Poison Control Centers
has a toll-free number that
automatically routes calls to
the nearest center:
1-800-222-1222.

Household Cleaners

Most liquid commercial household
cleaners release harmful vapors.
Store these with tight-fitting caps
and lids in a well-ventilated area
away from the kitchen and living
and sleeping areas. Always follow
instructions on the product label
for safe use and disposal. Keep the
phone number for your local poison
control center by the telephone,
and have the label handy to read
over the phone should an accidental
poisoning occur.

Paint

Store cans of paint in one place, upside down, with lids secured tightly.
Do not allow them to freeze. The
best disposal method is to use the
paint up or give it away to someone
who can use it, such as a theater
group. If a small amount of paint is
left in the can, open the lid and let
it air-dry in a well-ventilated area.
Wrap the can in newspapers and
put it out with the trash. Oil-based
paint must be taken to a hazardous
waste collection center.

Disposal

Americans generate an estimated 1.6 million tons of hazardous household waste per year. What becomes of it? The typical household dumps it down the drain, pours it on the ground, releases it into storm sewers, or throws it out with the trash. All these methods pose a threat to the quality of our water, our air, and our soil. Even empty containers of hazardous materials, which can retain chemical residue, pose hazards to sanitation workers, septic tanks, and wastewater treatment plants.

Experts believe that 5 to 15 percent of municipal solid waste contains hazardous substances.

Chemical Disposal

If a chemical product must be used, find out the best method for disposing of it. In most cases, the best thing to do is to use the product up (by sharing it with a friend, if necessary, or donating it to a business or organization).

If a product can be poured down the drain (see chart on pages 122–23), be sure to flush with plenty of water. If you have a septic system, this kind of waste will not pass through a treatment plant; it will either stick around your septic system or leach into the ground. Your local waste facility should be able to dispose of it instead.

Earth 911 provides tips and locations for disposing of and recycling all kinds of materials, from hazardous waste to electronics. Visit *www.earth911.org.*

Landfill Disposal

Products suitable for landfill disposal can go in the trash. Empty liquid containers can be thrown away, but only if fully drained — liquids should never be disposed of in the trash. When disposing of empty containers of toxic cleaners and polishes, wrap them in newspaper and throw them out with the trash. Some communities allow this disposal method for empty containers of indoor pesticides and fertilizers as well. Some products, like paint, are acceptable for landfill disposal if they are hardened or dried up. Contact local officials before throwing away any product you're concerned about.

Disposal of Large Items

Check with your local sanitation department on rules covering the disposal of large items. Big appliances, such as stoves, can often be hauled to your neighborhood Dumpster or left at the curb on certain days of the year, depending on where you live. Your area may have special rules on disposing of appliances that use CFC gas — specifically, air conditioners and refrigerators. If your local sanitation department doesn't collect large items, call your local solid waste agency to schedule a pickup, which comes with a charge. A landfill operator or scrap metal dealer may take appliances, also for a fee.

Computers

Be sure the contents of your hard drive are deleted first, to protect your privacy. Anything over 40 pounds should be taken to a regional collection center, which usually charges a small fee. Several companies will safely dispose of or recycle your computer; check out GreenDisk (*www.greendisk.com*), which accepts obsolete equipment

Hazardous Waste Disposal

This chart should be used only as a guide. Contact your local sanitation department to determine what disposal options exist in your area.

Automotive

Type of Product	Save for Collection	Reuse	Recycle	Trash	Flush
Antifreeze			●		
Auto Battery			●		
Brake Fluid	●				
Car Wax and Polish	●				
Degreaser	●				
Diesel Fuel	●		●		
Gasoline	●				
Kerosene	●		●		
Motor Oil			●		
Transmission Fluid	●				
Windshield Wiper Fluid	●				

Personal Care Products

Type of Product	Save for Collection	Reuse	Recycle	Trash	Flush
Aftershave / Perfume					●
Cosmetics				●	
Hair Permanent Lotions					●
Nail Polish (hardened)					●
Nail Polish	●				
Nail Polish Remover	●				
Prescription Medicines					●
Head Lice Shampoos	●				
Syringes (in sealed container)				●	

Cleaners

	F	T	RC	RU	SFC
Ammonia-based Cleaner	●				
Bleach-based Cleaner	●				
Disinfectant	●				●
Drain Cleaner	●				●
Floor Wax Stripper					●
Furniture Polish					●
Glass Cleaner	●				
Metal Cleaner					●
Oven Cleaner					●
Spot Cleaner					●
Toilet Bowl Cleaner	●				
Window Cleaner	●				

Home Improvement Products

	F	T	RC	RU	SFC
Adhesive and Glue (solvent-based)					●
Adhesive and Glue (water-based)		●			
Paint Brush Cleaner (solvent-based)				●	●
Paint (water-based latex)				●	●
Paint (solvent-based oil)				●	●
Paint Thinner				●	●
Paint Remover / Stripper					●
Putty / Grout / Caulk		●			
Stain and Varnish				●	●
Wood Preservative					●

Pesticides

	F	T	RC	RU	SFC
Fertilizer					●
Flea Collar and Spray					●
Fungus-control Chemicals					●
Insect-control Chemicals					●
Moth Balls					●
Rodent Poison					●
Weed Killer					●

Miscellaneous

	F	T	RC	RU	SFC
Aerosol Can		●			
Air Fresheners					
Air Freshener (used up)		●			●
Ammunition	contact law enforcement				
Artist and Hobby Paint			●		●
Batteries (alkaline)		●			
Batteries (NiCad or button)			●		●
Fabric Dye (concentrate)			●		●
Fabric Dye (diluted)	●				
Fireworks	soak in water, then trash				
Fluorescent Bulbs, Tubes, Ballast			●		●
Pool and Hot Tub Chemicals					●
Smoke Detector (ionizing)	return to manufacturer				
Thermometer (mercury)					●

for a small fee. Some computer makers — including Apple, Dell, Hewlett-Packard, and IBM — can recycle your machine, though some do so only when you buy a new one. See Resources (page 180) for contact information. Also, consider donating working equipment to charity; check your phone book for local organizations.

Toner and ink cartridges can be recycled; Staples and FedEx-Kinko's shops nationwide accept toner and ink, as do other businesses. (See *www.earth911.org* for local collection sites.)

For many hazardous products, no safe disposal method is available. These must be taken to a special collection facility or stored safely until your community holds a household hazardous waste collection day. Each community has different programs, so call your local environmental, health, or solid waste agency about programs and services in your area.

Hazardous Waste Don'ts

- Don't dump down storm sewers or in the backyard.

- Don't burn or bury.

- Don't put in the street or in a Dumpster.

- Don't put in the trash or pour down the drain before checking the disposal recommendation for that product.

- Don't reuse or share banned or restricted pesticides, prescription medicines, syringes, or products whose safety instructions are no longer readable.

Recycling

Taking out the trash isn't as simple as it used to be. Most communities now have recycling laws, yard waste laws, hazardous waste laws, and more. Your community probably has curbside pickup for recyclable glass, paper, plastic, cardboard, and metal containers, including aerosol cans. Bins are usually free, and sometimes multiple bins (which make sorting trash simpler) are provided at no charge. Communities without curbside pickup usually have a recycling station or drop-off location.

Collection Sites

Most communities also have collection sites for bulky items such as used tires, scrap wood and metal, computers and other electronic products, clothing, and textiles. In some places you can recycle leftover automotive supplies by taking them to an automotive service center, oil recycling station, or authorized collection site. Car and household batteries also can be turned in for recycling.

If you're confused about rules in your community, contact your city's municipal waste department to obtain a list of accepted items, requirements for disposal, and fees.

Or check out Earth 911 *(www.earth911.org)* for recycling tips about specific materials.

Recycling creates six times as many jobs as do land-filling and incineration.

Collection Containers

Place collection containers at source points in your home — bathroom, laundry room, garage, kitchen, home office, workshop — so you don't have to separate items later. Rinse out food containers and bottles, flatten aluminum cans to save space, remove plastic linings from cereal boxes, throw out caps and lids, and keep cardboard boxes dry. Pay attention to what goes in your recycling bins: An empty cereal box is usually fine. A greasy pizza box? Probably not.

The EPA estimates that 4.7 billion pounds of carpet enter the waste stream each year.

Donate

Donate electronics, toys, appliances, and other nonrecyclable items to charity or a thrift store. These organizations also accept clothing, furniture, books, and magazines. Be sure to make a list of your donations and their estimated worth and write them off on your income tax return. If you can't donate electronics locally, consider giving to a national nonprofit; the Environmental Protection Agency provides a guide at *www.plugintorecycling.org.*

Many UPS Stores and Mail Boxes Etc. locations accept foam packing peanuts. Big-box stores like Wal-Mart often have a recycling bin for plastic grocery bags. Collection sites for foam packaging (expanded polystyrene, or EPS) are listed at *www.epspackaging.org/info.html.*

Several carpet makers have reclamation programs. See Resources (page 180) for a list of companies.

Carpet America Recovery Effort is an industry and government initiative to prevent discarded carpet from overwhelming landfills. Visit *www.carpetrecovery.org* for more information.

The Rechargeable Battery Recycling Corporation website, *www.rbrc.org*, lists local collection sites. Old cell phones can be donated to charitable organizations; visit *www.charitablerecycling.com* for a local collection point. Many cell phone companies have recycling programs, too. (Be sure to deactivate your service first.)

Precycling & Freecycling

Prevent waste before it happens. Good purchasing decisions create less waste, making your recycling an easier, less troublesome task. Here are a few simple steps:

- Buy in bulk or in concentrate.

- Buy products that use less packaging.

- Use reusable cloth instead of paper.

- Use washable plastic and glass food containers, not Styrofoam.

- Use rechargeable batteries.

- Ask grocery store clerks to single-bag, not double-bag.

- Reduce junk mail by having your name removed from marketers' lists, via the Direct Marketers Assocation website, *www.dmaconsumers.org/consumerassistance.html*.

- Ask for and buy recycled products.

> ☼ **The following items do not belong in recycling bins: plastic grocery bags, Styrofoam, light bulbs, food-soiled paper, wax paper, ceramics.**

☼ **Gardening stores, catalogs, and websites sell attractive compost containers (from crockery to stainless steel) that will look great in any kitchen.**

One man's junk is another man's treasure. Freecycling, a grassroots movement run by local volunteers, can help you find someone who may be interested in your junk. If you have something you want to give away, check the postings for your area on *www.freecyle.org*. Craig's List (*www.craigslist.org*), a web-based community serving more than 50 cities, is another good place to find takers for your unwanted usable items.

Composting

When it comes to disposing of organic waste, a compost pile wins over a garbage disposal as the best green option. Garbage disposals use a significant amount of water and load sewage treatment plants and

septic tanks with organic matter. Composting returns organic matter to the earth. Adding compost to your lawn or garden nourishes plants and improves soil structure and water retention.

Much of what a typical household throws away is compostable. Collect kitchen waste in a compost bin or a bucket with a tight-fitting lid and bring it out to your backyard compost pile (or composter) every few days. Chopped-up scraps decompose quicker. Set up your compost pile in a well-drained, sunny spot. Keep it no larger than five feet square (or in diameter), so you have space to turn it and to remove the finished product.

A compost rule of thumb is three to four parts brown material (leaves, shredded newspapers) to one part green material (eggshells, coffee grounds, fruit and vegetable peelings). With proper watering, enough air, and a bit of turning, the mixture "cooks," heating up to about 140 degrees Fahrenheit, as microorganisms digest and break down the organic trash into what gardeners call "black gold."

Tips on getting your compost pile started can be found at *www.mastercomposter.com* and *www. vegweb.com/composting.*

Behold this compost! Behold it well!

– Walt Whitman, *Leaves of Grass*

Composting Don'ts

- Don't add meat, fish, bones, grease, cheese, or oily matter, which attract bugs and unwanted pests and take longer to decompose.

- Don't add weeds from the garden if they are going to seed.

- Don't add waste from carnivorous animals.

8 : RECIPES

YOU DON'T NEED INDUSTRIAL-STRENGTH
CHEMICALS TO CLEAN YOUR HOUSE.
NATURAL CLEANERS WORK JUST FINE
AND DON'T POLLUTE INDOOR AIR OR THE
WATER SUPPLY. WITH A FEW STAPLE
INGREDIENTS FROM THE GROCERY
STORE, PLUS SOME REUSABLE BOTTLES
AND JARS, YOU CAN REPLACE VIRTUALLY
EVERY COMMERCIAL CLEANING PRODUCT

YOU NOW DEPEND ON — FROM GENERAL CLEANERS TO FURNITURE POLISH TO SPOT REMOVERS.

A simple mixture of baking soda and water, for example, cleans sinks and countertops. Olive oil mixed with a bit of lemon juice polishes wood to a sparkling glow. Homemade cleaners not only do the job, they leave your house smelling fresh and clean. You can even tailor the scent, adding your favorite essential oils or fragrant hand-picked herbs. With make-it-yourself recipes, timely tips, and no-fail tricks, you'll find cleaning with home-made recipes to be an easy step to achieving a natural, green home.

Mixing it Up

Making your own cleaning products is quick, easy, and cheap. Most recipes require only one or two simple steps, are no-mess and no-fuss, and use ingredients you can get in one trip to the grocery store.

Because they're composed of mild, biodegradable ingredients, they may take a little longer to do the job, or require a bit more elbow grease, but these recipes really work. More important, they get the job done without polluting the environment or affecting your health.

You don't need to replace your entire cleaning cabinet with do-it-yourself recipes — start off by making just one or two replacements for commercial products, like a toilet bowl cleaner or an air freshener. As you become more familiar with the green approach, try more recipes — for spot removers, oven cleaner, dishwasher soap, and more.

These recipes work best when made fresh, but many keep indefinitely when stored properly. Keep bottles or jars of those right where you'll use them — in the laundry room, kitchen, bathroom, etc. (Don't forget to label them.)

Must-Have Recipes

These dozen recipes will replace nearly every commercial cleaning product in your cupboard.

All-Purpose Castile Cleaner, page 136. This pleasantly scented blend of vegetable-based soap and water cleans almost every surface in the home.

General Carpet Cleaner, page 137. This mix is good for spills or all-over cleaning.

Dishwasher and Laundry Soap, pages 138, 142. A dry mix that keeps both kitchenware and laundry clean.

Vinegar of the Four Thieves Disinfectant, page 138. This fragrant mix of vinegar and herbs is an old-fashioned remedy — and works wonders fighting germs.

Baking Soda–Based Drain Cleaner, page 139. With regular use, this simple cleaner will keep your drains clear.

Basic Floor Cleaner, page 140. Keeps every type of floor, from linoleum to hardwood, sparkling clean.

Lemon Furniture Polish, page 141. Toss out the oily spray and create your own fragrant mixture to pick up dust and leave your home smelling fresh and clean.

Natural Bleach, page 142. Replace one of the most toxic household chemicals with this easy-to-make mixture.

Baking Soda Oven Cleaner, page 144. No more smelly fumes with this natural oven cleaner.

Toilet Bowl Cleaner, page 144. Disinfect, clean, and deodorize without toxins.

Vinegar-Based Window Cleaner, page 145. Great-grandma's recipe for sparkling-clean windows.

Scouring Powder, page 145. A nontoxic substitute for harsher commercial products.

Chemistry 101

The basic chemistry of cleaning is pretty simple: It's all about acidity. Acidity is measured by pH, a scale that runs from 1 to 14. Neutral pH is 7; anything above that is alkaline, anything below is acidic. Typically, when you clean something, you are effectively neutralizing its pH. For an alkaline stain you use an acidic cleaner, and vice versa. Club soda, which is alkaline, will remove a coffee stain, which is acidic; vinegar, which is acidic, will neutralize alkaline stains such as water scale.

Caution:

Though it is used in many standard cleaners, ammonia should be avoided. It can damage the lungs when inhaled, and if accidentally mixed with bleach, it forms a toxic gas called chloramine. Most of the general cleaners listed here will replace any you use containing ammonia.

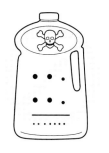

The Tools You Need

- Glass or stainless steel bowls
- Glass or stainless steel measuring cups
- Stainless steel measuring spoons
- Pumice stone
- Spray bottles, glass or plastic
- Squirt bottles, glass or plastic
- Shaker container with flip-top lid, or sugar shaker, glass or plastic
- Glass jars with tight-fitting lids
- Plastic or metal funnel
- Cotton or hemp cloths
- Cotton mops with wooden handles
- Natural sponges (see page 51)
- Whisk broom with natural bristles

All-Purpose Cleaners

Borax Cleaner

½   cup borax
1   gallon hot water
Pail or bucket

Mix all ingredients in the pail until borax is thoroughly dissolved. Use in areas that need general cleaning and wipe clean with a sponge or rag. You can also reduce the recipe to fit in a spray bottle for everyday use.

Shelf life: indefinite (in spray bottle)

Castile Cleaner

This cleaner works well on greasy stains.

1   teaspoon washing soda
2   teaspoons borax
½   teaspoon castile soap
2   cups hot water
10 drops essential oil
    of your choice
16 ounce spray bottle

Mix all ingredients in a spray bottle. (Add more washing soda to help whiten any stains.) Spray as needed and wipe clean with a natural sponge or cotton cloth.

Shelf life: indefinite

Scented Soap and Water

Don't forget the power of the basics.

2   cups hot water
1   to 2 ounces castile soap
5   to 10 drops essential oil
    of your choice
16 ounce spray bottle

Mix with a gentle shake in a spray bottle. Spray on counters, cupboards, or any surface that needs cleaning.

Shelf life: indefinite

Club Soda Spray

Sometimes the simplest of ingredients work the best.

2   cups club soda
16 ounce spray bottle
Funnel

Use a funnel to pour club soda into spray bottle. Spritz on area to be cleaned and wipe with a natural sponge or cotton cloth. Club soda is particularly good at removing acidic stains.

Shelf life: indefinite

Scented Vinegar Spray

Vinegar will fight mildew, while the essential oil minimizes the vinegary odor.

1   teaspoon borax
1   tablespoon castile soap
⅛   cup distilled white vinegar
2   cups hot water
5   to 10 drops essential oil
    of your choice
16 ounce spray bottle

Mix all ingredients in spray bottle. Spritz as needed and wipe with a natural sponge or cotton cloth. Good for drawing out dirt and for general cleaning.

Shelf life: indefinite

Scented Baking Soda

After using this mix, you'll need to thoroughly wipe surfaces with a damp rag or sponge to eliminate any residue.

Small box baking soda
10 drops essential oil of your choice
Shaker container with a flip-top lid,
    or a sugar shaker

Fill the shaker container half-full with baking soda; drop in essential oil and mix well with a fork. Add enough baking soda to fill the container and mix again with a fork. Sprinkle lightly on surfaces, then rub in lightly with a clean cotton cloth. It's best to test a small section first.

Shelf life: indefinite

General Appliance Cleaner

Dry baking soda shines up small appliances, such as toasters. It even removes bread wrappers that have been burned onto the toaster.

Baking soda
Sponge

Work baking soda into surface of appliances and wipe clean with warm water and a clean sponge.

Shelf life: indefinite

Carpet Cleaners & Deodorizers

Easy Deodorizer

Baking soda
Broom
Vacuum cleaner

Sprinkle baking soda over the carpet and leave on overnight. Sweep off as much as possible and vacuum the rest. Remember: Always spot-test on a hidden area before using any product on carpet.

Shelf life: indefinite

Easy Carpet Spill Absorber

Cornstarch or cornmeal
Broom
Vacuum cleaner

Pour cornstarch or cornmeal onto the spill; leave for 15 minutes. Sweep up as much as possible and vacuum the rest.

Shelf life: indefinite

General Carpet Cleaner

1   part liquid soap or detergent
1   part water

Whip together by hand or in a blender. Make at least one cup's worth. Sponge onto carpet, rub in, and wipe dry with a rag. Do section by section to make the job easier.

Shelf life: indefinite when kept in a sealed container, but rewhip the mixture before each use.

Dishwashing

Dishwasher Soap
1   part borax
1   part washing soda
Container (size of your choice)

Mix in the container and use in place
of commercial detergent. If you live in a
hard-water area, you may have to adjust
the proportions to avoid formation of
soap film on the dishes — try adding a
bit more soda if there is a film residue.

Shelf life: indefinite

Liquid Dishwashing Soap
Castile soap
Distilled white vinegar

Grate soap and add to dishwater. Add
vinegar to the rinsewater to give glasses
extra shine.

Shelf life: indefinite

Overnight Stain Remover
Baking soda
Shaker container

Sprinkle over dishes and let sit for at
least five minutes, or overnight. The
baking soda will cut down on odors and
loosen grime.

Shelf life: indefinite

Disinfectants

Vinegar of the Four Thieves
Legend has it that grave robbers during
a plague outbreak rubbed this on themselves to prevent illness.

2   quarts organic apple cider vinegar
Small handfuls of dried lavender,
    rosemary, sage, rue, mint
Large jar (about 2 quarts) with
    screw-top lid

Mix all ingredients in jar and cover tightly.
Let sit for at least four weeks and strain
out the herbs. Pour into a spray bottle.
Spray anywhere that's ripe for germs —
such as places where lots of hands have
touched, or in a sick room.

Shelf life: indefinite

Toilet Disinfectant
2   cups distilled white vinegar
a few drops essential oil of your choice
16 ounce spray bottle

Mix ingredients together and
spritz the toilet bowl as needed. Use a
toilet brush to swish mixture around the
sides of the bowl.

Shelf life: indefinite

General Antiseptic Spray

Liquid castile soap
10 to 20 drops lavender or tea tree
    essential oil
Funnel
16 ounce spray bottle

Mix together in a spray bottle and spritz as needed.

Shelf life: indefinite

Mildew Remover

Baking soda
Distilled white vinegar

Mix vinegar with water or sprinkle baking soda on a damp sponge to clean affected areas. Vinegar helps prevent mildew because acid kills mildew fungus.
Note: Proper ventilation and dehumidifiers can reduce or eliminate mildew and mold growth.

Shelf life: Use and discard.

Drain Cleaners

Baking Soda–Based Drain Cleaner

½ cup baking soda
½ cup salt
⅛ cup cream of tartar
Boiling water

Mix dry ingredients together and pour down the drain, followed by boiling water. Repeat until clear.

Shelf life: Use and discard.

Vinegar-Based Cleaner

½ cup baking soda
1 cup distilled white vinegar
Boiling water

Dissolve baking soda and vinegar in boiling water; pour the solution down the drain. Cover it with a drain plug for several minutes and flush with hot tap water until the clog breaks.

Shelf life: Use and discard.

Salt-Based Cleaner

½ cup salt
Boiling water

Pour salt down the drain, followed by boiling water; flush with hot tap water.

Shelf life: Use and discard.

Floors

Hardwood Floor Cleaner
¼ cup distilled white vinegar
1   gallon warm water
Pail or bucket

Mix ingredients in pail and mop wood
floors. After washing, rinse with water.
Don't leave large pools of water to dry.

Shelf life: Use and discard.

Linoleum and Vinyl Floor Cleaner
1   cup distilled white vinegar
2   gallons warm water
Club soda
Pail or bucket

Mix vinegar and water in pail and mop
floors; this mix is particularly good at
removing any greasy film. To remove
stains, rub club soda in with a clean
cotton cloth.

Shelf life: Use and discard.

Basic Floor Cleaner
⅛ cup liquid soap
⅛ cup distilled white vinegar
1   gallon water
10 drops essential oil of your choice
Pail or bucket

Combine all ingredients in pail;
use to mop any type of floor.

Shelf life: Use and discard.

Fresheners

Spicy Air Freshener
Water
Cloves
Cinnamon
Boiling water

Add spices to boiling water and let sim-
mer on the back of the stove; be sure
to remove from heat before the mixture
evaporates.

Shelf life: Use and discard.

Essential Oil Air Freshener
1   cup water
5   drops essential oil of your choice
Small spray bottle
Funnel

Mix the essential oil and water together
in the spray bottle and spritz in the
bathroom or kitchen, or in any room, to
freshen. Essential oils shouldn't leave
any stains or residue if mixed in proper
proportions.

Shelf life: indefinite

Baking Soda Deodorizing Spray
2   tablespoons baking soda
2   cups hot water
16 ounce spray bottle
Funnel

This formula neutralizes odors, rather than adding scents to the room. Mix baking soda and hot water together in a spray bottle until all baking soda is dissolved. Spritz as needed. There should be no residue left if the baking soda is well dissolved. If any residue occurs, simply wipe away with a clean cotton cloth.

Shelf life: indefinite

Odor Absorber
Baking soda

Sprinkle in trash cans and kitty litter pans. Put a fresh open box in the refrigerator to absorb odors there.

Shelf life: Use and discard.

Furniture Polish

Basic Furniture Polish No. 1
Vegetable-based liquid soap
Vegetable oil
Butcher's wax
Barely damp cloth

Dust furniture with a barely damp cloth. Clean wood floors and furniture with vegetable-based oil soaps. On unfinished wood, use vegetable oil to restore luster. Polish finished wood with butcher's wax once or twice a year.

Shelf life: indefinite if not mixed

Basic Furniture Polish No. 2
3   parts olive oil
1   part distilled white vinegar
Soft cloth

Mix olive oil and vinegar. Apply with soft cloth. Use this polish for deeper cleaning; for lighter jobs but for a fresher scent and deeper glow, try the Lemon Furniture Polish below.

Shelf life: Use and discard.

Lemon Furniture Polish
2   cups olive, vegetable,
     or mineral oil
Juice of 1 lemon

Mix oil with lemon juice. Apply with a soft cloth and buff until you can see your reflection.

Shelf life: Use and discard.

Laundry

Basic Laundry Detergent
1 part borax
1 part washing soda
Container (size of your choice)

Mix in a container and use in place of
commercial detergent. If you live in a
hard-water area, you may have to add
a bit more soda.

Shelf life: indefinite

Starch
1 tablespoon cornstarch
1 pint cold water
Small spray bottle

Dissolve cornstarch in water. Place the solution in a spray bottle. Shake before using.

Shelf life: indefinite

Natural Bleach
¼ cup washing soda or borax

Add to each laundry load with the wash
cycle to whiten whites and brighten colors.

Shelf life: indefinite

Natural Whitener
1 cup fresh lemon juice
Half-filled bucket of water

Add lemon juice to water and soak
clothes overnight.

Shelf life: Use and discard.

All-Purpose Stain Remover
This recipe works well on blood, choco-
late, coffee, mildew, mud, and urine.

¼ cup borax
2 cups cold water
Soaking pail

Mix the borax and cold water together
and soak stained clothing. Wash as usual.

Shelf life: Use and discard.

Metals

All-Purpose Metal Cleaner
Wood ashes

With a damp rag, rub wood ashes onto metal and polish. Rinse well with hot water and dry with a fresh cloth.

Shelf life: Use and discard.

Toothpaste-Based Metal Cleaner
Toothpaste

With your hand, rub regular toothpaste into the metal; polish with a clean rag.

Shelf life: Use and discard.

Metal-Tarnish Remover
Distilled white vinegar

Soak metal in vinegar and rinse clean; wipe with a soft rag.

Shelf life: Use and discard.

Silver-Tarnish Remover
Handful salt
Water
Aluminum container

Dissolve salt in water in an aluminum container and add silver; let it soak 5 to 10 minutes (or longer if necessary). The saltwater will magnetize the tarnish away. Remove silver and rub with a clean cotton cloth.

Shelf life: Use and discard.

Copper and Brass Cleaner
Handful salt
Distilled white vinegar

Add enough vinegar to salt to make a paste. Apply the mixture to copper surfaces with a rag and rub clean. Adding a handful of all-purpose flour makes a less abrasive cleaner.

Shelf life: Use and discard.

Stainless Steel Cleaner I
Baking soda or mineral oil
Distilled white vinegar

Use baking soda or mineral oil, and shine with a damp cloth, and use vinegar to remove spots.

Shelf life: Use and discard.

Stainless Steel Cleaner II
Cream of tartar
Hydrogen peroxide

Make a paste of 3 parts cream of tartar and one part hydrogen peroxide. Rub the paste on rust stains with a damp cloth; wipe clean after it has dried.

Shelf life: Use and discard.

Leather

Natural Leather Polish

1 ¼ cups linseed oil
1 ¼ cups distilled white vinegar

Boil linseed oil. Let cool and add vinegar. Apply with a cloth, then buff with a clean cloth.

Shelf life: Use and discard.

Oven Cleaners

Oven Spill Remover

Salt

Let the oven cool, then sprinkle salt on the spill right away. Let it cool for a few more minutes, then scrape the spill away and wash the area clean.

Shelf life: Use and discard.

Baking Soda Oven Cleaner

Baking soda
Water

Sprinkle the oven with baking soda and spray with water. Let it sit for several hours or overnight; scrape up stains and spills. Be sure to thoroughly wash the oven with water.

Shelf life: Use and discard.

Tub, Tile and Toilet Cleaners

Toilet Bowl Cleaner

Baking soda
Distilled white vinegar
Washing soda

Sprinkle the toilet bowl with baking soda. Drizzle with vinegar; scour with a toilet brush. This not only cleans, it deodorizes. Or, use soap and washing soda to clean, baking soda to freshen.

Shelf life: Use and discard.

Toilet Bowl Stain Remover

Pumice stone

Thoroughly wet the pumice stone and rub on spots until they disappear.

Shelf life: indefinite

Basin, Tub, and Tile Cleaner

Half a lemon
Borax

Dip the lemon half in borax and rub on the area to be cleaned. Rinse surface and dry with a soft cloth.

Shelf life: Use and discard.

Windows

Vinegar-Based Window Cleaner
2   teaspoons distilled white vinegar
1   quart warm water
Spray bottle (size of your choice)

Mix all ingredients well. Spritz on windows and use a natural linen towel or other soft cloth to clean. If necessary, use rubbing alcohol to clean wax left from commercial glass cleaners.

Shelf life: indefinite

Scouring Powder
Baking soda or borax

Lightly sprinkle on surface to clean; wipe with a sponge. Rinse well.

Shelf life: indefinite

Cornstarch-Based Window Cleaner
½   cup cornstarch
2   quarts warm water
Pail or bucket

Mix well and apply with a sponge, then wipe windows dry with absorbent cloth or old towels. This solution is great for car windows and bathroom mirrors, leaving them shiny and streak-free.

Shelf life: Use and discard.

Tile Cleaner
¼   cup distilled white vinegar
1   gallon water
10 drops essential oil
Pail or bucket

Mix well and use a sponge or rag to clean. This removes most dirt without scrubbing and doesn't leave a film.

Shelf life: Use and discard.

Club Soda Window Cleaner
Club soda
Spray bottle (size of your choice)

Spritz on windows; wipe clean.

Shelf life: indefinite

Soft Scrubber
½   cup baking soda
Liquid castile soap
10 drops essential oil

Add enough soap to baking soda to make a creamy mixture. Use a sponge to apply and clean; rinse the surface well.

Shelf life: Use and discard.

Chapter

9 : STAIN GUIDE

IT IS THE NATURE OF THINGS THAT
YOU WILL SPILL COFFEE ON YOUR
FRESH WHITE BLOUSE, YOUR SON WILL
COME HOME WITH GRASS STAINS ON HIS
KHAKI PANTS, AND YOUR NEIGHBOR
WILL OVERTURN A GLASS OF RED WINE
ON YOUR NEW SOFA. BUT ALL IS NOT
LOST. MOST STAINS CAN BE REMOVED IF
TREATED IMMEDIATELY AND WITH PROPER

CARE. YOUR HIGH-SCHOOL CHEMISTRY TEACHER ALWAYS SAID THAT HER CLASS WOULD BE USEFUL, AND SHE WAS RIGHT. WHEN IT COMES TO TREATING EVEN THE TOUGHEST STAINS, IT'S ALL A MATTER OF SCIENCE.

Almost every stain falls into one of a few categories: non-water-soluble, oily or fatty, protein-based, and tannin- or glucose-based. Each of these types of stains responds to different techniques and products. For example, tannin and glucose stains are best treated by mildly alkaline products (such as baking soda); non-water-soluble stains will resist regular soap and water, but should be easy to manage with a solvent-based cleaner. In addition to the remedies detailed here, there are several nontoxic stain removers available; they are often enzyme-based and work well to remove many different kinds of stains. See the Product Guide, page 163, for recommendations.

Dealing with Stains

Dealing with stains on clothing and linens is much different than treating stains on carpet and upholstery — you can't throw a sofa in the wash. As with clothing, though, you can remove most stains on furniture or rugs if you tackle them as soon as possible. Keep several bottles of club soda on hand, as it is a great first line of defense against many different stains. The Product Guide includes stain removers and carpet cleaners that will help out as well.

Non-Water-Soluble Stains
(includes crayon, hand lotion, cosmetics, shoe polish, and ball-point pen ink). As the category name indicates, these stains cannot be tackled with soap and water — and are the most difficult to remove (in the case of ballpoint pen ink, almost impossible). They require solvents, such as rubbing alcohol, acetone, or nail polish remover. Some nail polish removers contain aloe vera or other moisturizing ingredients; avoid them. Solvent cleaners are usually not environmentally safe, but may be the only way to remove stubborn non-water-soluble stains. Use them only in rooms with good ventilation.

Protein Stains
(includes egg, blood, vomit, and ice cream). If treated correctly, protein stains can be easily removed. Don't use hot water on these stains; heat can permanently set them. The best approach: cold water and an enzyme-based stain remover. Many laundry detergents and soaps have enzymes (including several listed in our Product Guide) as does meat tenderizer. If you are worried about odor from a stain, blot with a one-to one mixture of distilled white vinegar and cold water.

Fatty and Oily Food Stains
(includes cheese, ketchup, choco-late, cream, mayonnaise, milk, and salad dressing). Most fatty and oily

food stains can be treated with a little soap and water. They have a low acidity and react well to alkaline cleaners such as borax, baking soda, and mild liquid soaps. Often the best way to treat this kind of stain is to cover the spot with a mixture of borax and warm water and let it sit (for at least 20 minutes and up to two hours), then rinse with cold water.

Tannin and Glucose Stains (includes beer, wine, and other alcoholic beverages, berries, black coffee, fruit juice, tea, and tobacco). Tannin and glucose stains are best treated with a mild laundry detergent or soap. Some of these stains can be very difficult to remove, especially if they are left to sit. Treat coffee, tea, and red wine stains immediately.

Stain Tips

☀ Don't wait. Treat stains when they're fresh; a set stain may never come out.

☀ Blot, never rub. This will spread the stain around and cause the fabric to absorb it.

☀ Know what you're cleaning. Read the care label on clothing or fabric; see page 106.

☀ Be careful with heat and hot water. Many protein-based stains will be set by hot water or heat (from an iron, for example).

☀ Test your fabric. Some fabrics will discolor if treated with harsh stain removers. Try your stain-removing technique on a snip of fabric or on a place that is not visible.

☀ Check before tumble-drying. Inspect any stain-treated garment before you put it in the dryer. If the stain is still visible after one wash cycle, retreat and launder again.

☀ Be patient. It can take time for a stain to respond to treatment.

☀ Know your limits. Some fabrics, such as leather, suede, and silk, require professional treatment.

Stain-Fighting Tool Kit

Baking soda
Borax
Carpet cleaner ☀
Club soda
Cream of tartar
Distilled white vinegar
Eucalyptus oil
Glycerin
Hydrogen peroxide (3 percent)
Lemon juice
Meat tenderizer (unseasoned)
Mild liquid dish soap ☀
Nail polish remover (acetone)
Rubbing alcohol
Salt
Soda siphon
Spoon or dull knife
Spray bottles
Stain remover ☀
Talcum powder
White paper towels or
   white terry cloth towels

☀ See the Product Guide for
   green recommendations

Stain-by-Stain

Adhesive Tape Residue
Clothing and linens: Harden the sticky surface with ice in a plastic bag and scrape any residue with a dull knife. Cover area with a stain remover and let stand for an hour. Rinse, then launder. Upholstery and Carpet: Harden the sticky surface with ice and scrape any residue with a dull knife. Blot spots with acetone nail polish remover. If the spot remains, treat with a carpet cleaner.

Beer
Clothing and linens: Blot the stain with a one-to-eight solution of distilled white vinegar and water. If that doesn't completely remove the stain, treat with a stain remover and launder as usual. Upholstery and carpet: Sponge up any excess liquid. Saturate affected part of the carpet or upholstery with a one-to-one solution of distilled white vinegar and water. Blot the area with a cool, damp towel. If any discoloration remains, treat it with a carpet cleaner.

Berries/Red Fruit Juices
Clothing and Linens: Pour boiling water directly over the stain (this is not a good method for delicate fabrics). Or, treat the stain immediately with fresh lemon juice. If the stain has already set, try blotting with glycerin and letting it sit for 30 minutes, then rinsing the

fabric clean with warm water and allow to air dry. Launder as usual. Upholstery and carpet: Wipe up any excess residue. Blot with mild laundry detergent and warm water. Rinse the spot with a one-to-one mixture of distilled white vinegar and water, blot again with mild detergent and water, then sponge clean with cold water.

Blood

Clothing and linens: In a sink, soak freshly stained garments in a mixture of salt (about a handful) and cold water for 30 minutes. Do not use warm or hot water — they can set the stain. If the stain has set, try covering it with a paste made of unseasoned meat tenderizer and warm water. Leave it for 15 to 20 minutes, then rinse with cold water. Launder as usual. Upholstery and carpet: Blot a fresh stain continuously with cold water until it disappears. If this doesn't work, try treating it with a carpet cleaner. Treat dried stains with a small amount of glycerin; let stand for 30 minutes, then blot with water.

Candle Wax

Clothing and linens: Harden the wax with an ice cube and then remove it with a dull knife. Place a flattened brown paper bag atop the stained area and press with a warm iron to allow the wax to melt into the paper. Treat any remain-ing stain with rubbing alcohol or a stain remover. Launder as usual. Upholstery and carpet: Allow the wax to harden completely, then scrape off as much as possible. Place a flattened brown paper bag over the remaining stain and press with a warm iron until the wax melts into the paper. Move the bag around to prevent excess wax from transferring back onto the carpet, or upholstery.

Chewing Gum

Clothing and linens: Harden the gum with an ice cube (or put the garment in the freezer), then scrape the gum off with a dull knife. Treat with a stain remover and launder as usual. Soaking the garment in distilled white vinegar before washing can help loosen any remaining gum.
Upholstery and carpet: Apply a plastic bag of ice cubes to the chewing gum so that it hardens. Carefully remove the hardened residue with a dull knife. Clean any remaining residue or stain with carpet cleaner.

Chocolate

Clothing and linens: If the stain is fresh, soak fabric in cold water; if it persists after soaking, blot with a mild laundry detergent or soap to remove any excess residue. If the stain has set, treat it with stain remover and launder as usual. Upholstery and carpet: Allow melted chocolate to harden and then scrape off with a dull knife. Blot stain with a mixture of mild detergent and warm water.

Coffee

Clothing and linens: Rinse the stain immediately with warm water, then let the fabric soak in a borax and water solution. Blot affected area with a stain remover, let sit for 30 minutes and launder as usual. If the stain has set, try the method recommended for treating dried tea stains (see page 157). Upholstery and carpet: Blot the stain with paper towels, then spray with a one-to-three solution of water and distilled white vinegar. Blot, then apply a mixture of liquid dish soap and water. Blot again and rinse with cold water. If the stain has set, professional treatment may be necessary.

Crayons

Crayon is not water-soluble; you'll probably need to use some sort of solvent. Crayola recommends WD-40, though it's not a green product. Heat (from a blow dryer) can help. Clothing and linens: Scrape off excess crayon with a dull knife, then apply a small amount of rubbing alcohol to the stain and blot. Rinse, apply a small amount of liquid dish soap to the stain, then blot with a damp towel. Launder as usual.

Upholstery and carpet: Remove excess crayon with a dull knife. Apply rubbing alcohol to the stain with a white towel and blot the stain until no more color is transferred to the towel. Walls: Try heating the marks with a blow dryer and then wiping off the loosened crayon. Rubbing with a baking soda and water paste works, too, and is gentle enough to use on most wall coverings and paint.

Fruit Juice

Clothing and linens: Blot with a mixture of distilled white vinegar and water, then apply a stain remover. If the stain has dried, treat it first with a small amount of glycerin, letting it stand for one hour. Rinse, then launder as usual. Upholstery and carpet: Gently blot with a mixture of mild laundry detergent and warm water. Rinse the spot with a sponge dipped in a one-to-one mixture of distilled white vinegar and water (do not soak the spot). Repeat both steps until the stain disappears. Sponge with cold water to rinse.

Grape Juice

Clothing and linens: Sprinkle with salt, to break up and absorb the stain. Soak the garment in cold water. If the stain remains, treat with a stain remover and launder as usual. Upholstery and carpet: Blot up any excess liquid with a paper towel. Pour club soda on the stain and let it sit for five minutes. Blot the stain with a white towel until no more color appears on the towel. Sponge with cold water to rinse.

Grass

Clothing and linens: Do not use ammonia or degreasers — they can make stains permanent. Blot with a little rubbing alcohol, then rinse with water. Apply liquid dish soap to the stain, rinse with water, and allow the garment to air dry. Launder as usual. If discoloration remains, soak the garment in warm water with a stain remover for 30 to 60 minutes. Relaunder in hot water. Upholstery and carpet: Pour a small amount of mild laundry detergent onto the stain and let it stand for two hours. Blot the soap away using a damp towel.

Grease (including motor oil, butter, fat, cooking oil, and salad dressing)

Clothing and linens: Blot excess grease with paper towels, then sprinkle with talcum powder to absorb any remaining grease. Treat with a stain remover, then launder. For delicate fabric, dab the stain with a little eucalyptus oil, then hand wash. Upholstery and carpet: Dab with a small amount of liquid laundry detergent; let it stand for a few hours. Scrub clean with a small brush. Wipe away any residue with a damp white towel.

Ink (ballpoint)

Clothing and linens: Alcohol can dissolve ballpoint ink. Bic, the pen manufacturer, recommends using an alcohol-based hair spray; spray, blot, and then launder. You can also saturate the stain with rubbing alcohol, making sure there is a white towel underneath the stain to collect the excess ink. Rinse the garment thoroughly before laundering. Upholstery and carpet: Press a paper towel to the stain to absorb as much of it as possible. Apply rubbing alcohol and blot. Walls: Spray alcohol-based hair spray directly on the ink, then wipe with a paper towel or cloth rag. Repeat until the stain is gone.

Ketchup

Clothing and linens: Rinse with cold water, then let the garment soak in a solution of liquid laundry detergent or soap and cold water. Rinse, apply a stain remover, and launder as usual. If stain remains, try treating with a one-to-one solution of distilled white vinegar and water, reapplying stain remover, and relaundering. Upholstery and carpet: Make a thick paste of borax and water. Apply directly to the stain and allow it to sit for 30 minutes. Wipe the paste away and blot with a damp towel.

Lipstick

Lipstick leaves a difficult, oily stain; professional treatment may be necessary. Clothing and linens: Place the stain face down on a white towel and apply a stain remover. Move the towel around so residue doesn't transfer back to the garment. Rinse, apply more stain remover directly to any remaining discoloration, then launder. Upholstery and carpet: Wipe away any excess lipstick. Wet the stain with a small amount of rubbing alcohol. Blot with a white towel until no stain is transferred to the towel. Treat with a carpet cleaner or spot remover if a blemish remains.

Milk

Clothing and linens: Rinse with warm water, treat with a stain remover, then launder as usual. Upholstery and carpet: A forgotten milk spill can leave a smell that is very difficult to remove. Dab fresh stains with a sponge and warm water, then apply a carpet cleaner. Use the same approach with upholstered furniture; treat any remaining spots with a stain remover or carpet cleaner.

Mustard

Mustard stains require particularly quick action; once dried they can be almost impossible to remove. This treatment can also be used on curry stains. Clothing

and linens: Rinse with cold water and dab with liquid dish soap. If the discoloration remains or the stain is already set, apply a little glycerin directly to the stain and let it stand for 30 minutes. Rinse the glycerin off with a one-to-one mixture of distilled white vinegar and cold water. Launder as usual. Upholstery and carpet: Immediately scrape away any residue. Blot the stain with a few drops of distilled white vinegar; let the vinegar sit for a few minutes, then blot with cold water to rinse.

Nail Polish

Clothing and linens: Slowly blot with a white towel dipped in rubbing alcohol until the stain fades. Apply a stain remover to any remaining spot, let it sit for 30 minutes, and then launder as usual. If the fabric is colorsafe and alcohol does not take care of the stain, try using an acetone nail polish remover. Upholstery and carpet: Blot with a white towel dipped in rubbing alcohol. Apply a carpet cleaner to any remaining spot. If alcohol does not work and the upholstery or carpet is color-safe, try using an acetone nail polish remover.

Paint (latex-base)

Clothing and linens: Rinse stain in warm water while paint is still wet; dried latex paint is difficult to remove. The best method for dried latex paint is to treat it with a water-soluble paint or varnish remover and then rinse the fabric thoroughly. Launder as usual. Upholstery and carpet: Wipe or scrape away any excess paint. Mix a teaspoon of mild liquid laundry detergent with warm water and blot. Rinse by blotting the spot with clean water. If any discoloration remains, apply a carpet cleaner. If the paint has dried, try treating it with water-soluble paint or varnish remover.

Paint (oil-base)
Oil-base paint is more difficult to remove than latex; again, it's best to act immediately. Clothing and linens: Treat the stain with rubbing alcohol, then soak the fabric in equal parts hot distilled white vinegar and milk for several hours. Rinse the fabric thoroughly and launder as usual. Upholstery and carpet: Wipe away any excess paint (or scrape away dry paint with a dull knife). Use a white towel moistened with rubbing alcohol to blot the stain until no more color shows up on the towel.

Perspiration
Clothing and linens: Treat new stains with an enzyme-based stain remover and launder as usual. If the stain is older, soak the garment in a solution of distilled white vinegar and water, rinse, and launder in hot water. A nonchlorine bleach will help restore whites.

Red Wine
Clothing and linens: Immediately blot the stain with a white towel soaked in club soda. (If you have a siphon, spray the garment with the club soda.) If the stain persists, soak the garment in a borax solution, then rinse and launder as usual. If the stain has set, follow the directions for dried tea stains. Upholstery and carpet: On carpet, apply club soda, blot dry, then treat any remaining stain with a carpet cleaner. If that doesn't fully remove it, apply glycerin and let it sit for up to an hour. Sponge off with cold water. For fresh stains on furniture, sponge with warm water. If there is still discoloration, cover the damp spot with talcum powder, let it sit for a few minutes, then brush away using a soft cloth. Treat set stains with glycerin.

Rust
Clothing and linens: Dampen spot with some water and cover with cream of tartar. Steam the fabric by holding it over a pot of boiling water. Rinse well with cold water; the stain should fade as you rinse. Launder as usual. Upholstery and carpet: Commercial rust removers work, but they can be caustic. A green alternative: Cover the stain with lemon juice (either fresh or bottled), then sprinkle with salt. Let the mixture stand for an hour, then sponge off with clean water.

Tea

Clothing and linens: Dried tea stains on fabric call for special treatment. Cassandra Kent's book *Household Hints and Tips* offers a great solution: Drape the fabric over a bowl or basin. Sprinkle with laundry borax until the whole stain is thickly covered. Pour a pot of hot water around the stain, working toward the center. Repeat treatment as necessary; launder as usual. (Do not use this method on delicate fabrics, as the hot water can be damaging.)

Upholstery and carpet: On carpet, blot a fresh stain with a paper towel and then sponge with warm water. Treat the spot with a bit of carpet cleaner. On furniture, sponge the stain with a borax and water solution, then wipe with a damp cloth. If spot remains, treat with a stain remover.

Tomato

Clothing and linens: Rinse the stain with cold water, then blot with a mixture of water and distilled vinegar. Rinse, apply a stain remover, and launder as usual. Upholstery and carpet: Remove any excess residue with a paper towel. Apply a small amount of rubbing alcohol to the stain and blot with a white towel until no more color is transferred to the towel.

Urine

Clothing and linens: Soak in a solution of distilled white vinegar and hot water (or cold water if the fabric is delicate) for 30 minutes. Rinse the garment in clean water and launder as usual.

Upholstery and carpet: *The Naturally Clean Home* has a great tip for removing urine stains from carpet: Blot with paper towels to remove as much of the liquid as possible. With a sponge, apply a solution of one quarter cup vinegar, a teaspoon of liquid dish soap, and several drops of eucalyptus oil. Let the mixture stand for 20 to 30 minutes, then blot again using a clean, damp towel.

Vomit

Clothing and linens: Wipe away any remaining residue. Rub the stained fabric together between your hands gently while holding the garment under a stream of cold water. Treat with a stain remover and then launder as usual.

Upholstery and carpet: Wipe up any remaining residue. Sponge with a mix of laundry borax and water, then with cold water. Treat any remaining stain with a carpet cleaner.

10 : PRODUCT GUIDE

GREEN CLEANING PRODUCTS ARE EASIER TO FIND THAN EVER. SOME BRANDS ARE STOCKED AT THE SUPERMARKET, GROCERY, OR BIG-BOX RETAILER, AND MANY MORE ARE AVAILABLE AT SPECIALTY SHOPS AND HEALTH FOOD STORES. THE WEB IS A GREAT SOURCE, TOO, WITH SITES THAT OFFER A WIDE SELECTION OF GOODS, OFTEN AT DISCOUNT PRICES.

MANY OF THESE PRODUCTS ARE NO MORE EXPENSIVE THAN THEIR NON-GREEN ALTERNATIVES. THE FOLLOWING IS A LIST OF THE BEST GREEN CLEANING PRODUCTS AVAILABLE, AS WELL AS INFORMATION ON PRICES, QUANTITY, AND WHERE TO BUY THEM.

One of the flaws of traditional cleaning products is that they do not list their ingredients, so it's difficult to determine which products are harmful and which ones are safe. There are some good sources of information about cleaning products, though. The National Library of Medicine's Household Products Database (*www.house holdproducts.nlm.nih.gov*) collects manufacturers' information. *The Safe Shopper's Bible* is a comprehensive guide to nontoxic cleaners and other household products. The Green Guide (*www.thegreenguide.com*) has a section dedicated to product reviews and includes a detailed list of nontoxic cleaning products.

The Basics

One common thread to green cleaning is to keep it simple. Most of our cleaning tasks can be handled without newly manufactured chemicals and ultraspecific products. And at the heart of many green solutions to cleaning problems are just a few ingredients: baking soda, soap, and vinegar. These three ingredients are nearly universal, but name brands can sometimes deliver more consistent quality. Castile soap can be difficult to find in stores, but it's worth the search. Look for it at health food stores and online.

Baking Soda
Arm and Hammer
Baking Soda
16 oz. box, $1.29*
12 oz. shaker, $.99

Castile Soap
Dr. Bronner's Liquid
Castile Soap
8 oz. bottle, $5.75

Kirk's Castile Bar Soap
4 oz. bar, $2

Kirk's Castile Liquid
Soap
16 oz. bottle, $6.25

Vermont Liquid
Castile Soap
8 oz. bottle, $4.99

Vinegar
Heinz Distilled White
Vinegar
32 oz. bottle, $1.09

Washing Soda
Arm & Hammer Super
Washing Soda
3.7 lbs. box, $2

* Prices quoted here reflect advertised or retail costs as of March 2007. Your cost may vary.

Laundry

The cleaning products that you use to do your laundry need to be able to get out the toughest stains, take care of the most delicate fabrics, and keep whites from looking dingy. Conventional detergents and bleaches can be some of the most dangerous products in your home. For instance, many liquid detergents are made with ethoxylated alcohols, which contain the carcinogen 1,4-dioxane. Look for laundry detergents that are vegetable-based, not petroleum-based, and replace your chlorine bleach with a safer, more environmentally friendly hydrogen peroxide–based bleach.

Bleach

Bi-O-Kleen Oxygen
Bleach Plus
32 oz., $5.99

Earth Friendly
Oxo-Brite
Non-Chlorine Bleach
3.6 lbs., $10.49

Ecover Natural
Non-Chlorine
Bleach Ultra
64 oz., $5.19

Naturally Yours
Natural Bleach
32 oz., $6

Shaklee Nature Bright
All-Fabric Laundry
Brightener
32 oz., $10.75

Delicates

Ecover Natural
Delicate Wash
32 oz., $4.89

Fabric Softener

Ecover Natural Fabric
Softener
32 oz., $4.59

Mrs. Meyer's Fabric
Softener
32 oz., $7.99

Seventh Generation
Fabric Softener,
Natural Lavender
Scent
40 oz., $5.99

Shaklee Softer than
Soft Fabric Softener
16 oz., $10.15

Sun and Earth Ultra
Fabric Softener
40 oz., $5.99

Ironing Sprays

Caldrea Linen Spray
32 oz., $12

Mrs. Meyer's Ironing
Spray
16 oz., $4.99

Laundry Soap &
Detergent

Bi-O-Kleen Laundry
Liquid
64 oz., $10.99

Cal Ben Seafoam
All Temperature
Laundry Soap
1 gallon (powder), $20

Earth Friendly ECOS
Powder Laundry
Detergent
54 oz., $6.99

Ecover Natural
Laundry Powder Ultra
48 oz., $7.99

Method Laundry
Detergent-Bleach
Alternative
32 oz., $8

Seventh Generation
Laundry Liquid,
Free and Clear
50 oz., $8.39

Sun and Earth Deep
Cleaning Formula
Laundry Detergent
50 oz. (powder), $5.99

Stain Removers &
Pre-Wash

Bi-O-Kleen Bac-Out
Stain and Odor
Eliminator
32 oz., $8.39

Bio Pac Laundry
Liquid
32 oz., $6.29

Earth Friendly Zainz
Laundry Pre-Wash
6 oz., $3.59

Ecover Natural Stain
Remover
6.8 oz., $3.79

Naturally Yours All-
Purpose Fabric Spotter
32 oz., $8

Dishwashing

Whether you use a dishwasher or wash your dishes by hand, there are numerous products that make this daily chore more environmentally friendly. Avoid dishwashing detergents that contain chlorine bleach or phosphates. As with laundry detergents, seek out liquid dishwashing soap that is vegetable-based, not petroleum-based.

Automatic Dishwasher Soap

Bi-O-Kleen Automatic Dish Soap
32 oz., $8.79

Cal Ben "Destain" Automatic Dish Machine Compound
1.5 lbs., $10

Ecover Tablets
24 tablets, $5.89

Seventh Generation Automatic Dishwashing Gel
45 oz., $6.49

Shaklee Basic D Automatic Dishwashing Concentrate
32 oz., $10.95

Liquid Soap

Bio Pac Dishwashing Liquid
22 oz., $5.39

Cal Ben Seafoam Liquid Dish Soap
16 oz., $8

Earth Friendly Dishmate
25 oz., $2.89

Mrs. Meyer's Dish Soap Liquid
16 oz., $4.99

Seventh Generation Dish Liquid
25 oz., $2.99

Sun and Earth Ultra Dishwashing Liquid
25 oz., $3.79

Rinse Aids

Earth Friendly Wave Jet
8 oz., $3.99

Ecover Rinse
16 oz., $4.69

Surface Cleaners

There is nothing quite like cleaning a messy stove top, wiping through the dirt on a windowpane, or scrubbing a countertop until it shines. However, the usual surface cleaners that help you accomplish these jobs emit dangerous fumes and can leave harmful residue. There are many products that use natural ingredients, such as citrus and vinegar, to clean and degrease effectively without caustic chemicals. Avoid products that use ammonia, which is a respiratory irritant, and ethyl cellosolve, which is a neurotoxin.

All-Purpose Cleaners

Caldrea All-Purpose Cleaner
32 oz., $12

Earth Friendly Parsley All-Purpose Kleener
22 oz., $5.09

Lifekind All-Purpose Cleaner Concentrate
16 oz., $8.95

Mrs. Meyer's All-Purpose Cleaner
32 oz., $7.99

Shaklee Basic H Squared
16 oz., $11.95

Vermont Soaps Liquid Sunshine Non Toxic Cleaner
38 oz., $12.98

Cream Scrub

Bi-O-Kleen Soy Blends Soy Cream Cleanser
32 oz., $5.59

Earth Friendly Cream Cleanser
16 oz., $3.09

Ecover Natural Cream Scrub Non-Scratching
16 oz., $2.79

Hope's Cooktop Cleaning Cream
10 oz., $5.95

Degreaser

Bi-O-Kleen All-Purpose Cleaner Degreaser
32 oz., $6.99

Citra-Solv Natural Cleaner and Degreaser
16 oz., $10.45

Naturally Yours
Degreaser
32 oz., $7

Seventh Generation
Citrus Cleaner &
Degreaser
32 oz., $5.49

Shaklee Scour Off
9 oz. paste, $8.35

Glass Cleaners

Bi-O-Kleen Glass
Cleaner
32 oz., $4.99

Caldrea Window Spray
16 oz., $8

Ecover Glass and
Surface Cleaner
16 oz., $4

Mrs. Meyer's Window
Spray
20 oz., $4.99

Seventh Generation
Glass & Surface
Cleaner Free & Clear
32 oz., $5.39

Sun and Earth Glass
Cleaner
22 oz., $3.79

Scrub Powders

Bon Ami Cleaning
Powder
12 oz., $1.49

Caldrea Powdered
Scrub
11 oz., $8

Mrs. Meyer's Surface
Scrub
12 oz., $4.99

20 Mule Team Borax
(also a laundry powder)
4 lbs., $4

Bathroom

Bathroom cleaning products can be some of the most caustic on the market. Perhaps the biggest offenders are toilet bowl cleaners, which often contain sodium hydroxide (lye). As with surface cleaners, avoid products with ammonia or chlorine bleach, and seek out products that use natural, vegetable-based ingredients. Take heart: You shouldn't need toxic cleaners to rid your bathroom of mold, mildew, and odors.

Toilet Cleaners

Bi-O-Kleen Soy Blends
Soy Toilet Scrub
32 oz., $5.59

Earth Friendly Toilet
Bowl Cleaner
24 oz., $3.10

Ecover Natural Toilet
Bowl Cleaner, Thick
Formula
25 oz., $3.99

Seventh Generation
Toilet Bowl Cleaner,
Natural Mint
32 oz., $5.39

Shower Cleaners

Earth Friendly Shower
Kleener
22 oz., $4.69

Method Daily Shower
Cleaner
28 oz., $4.99

Mrs. Meyer's Shower
Cleaner
22 oz., $4.99

Seventh Generation
Shower Cleaner
32 oz., $5.39

Tub & Tile Cleaners

Enviro-Magic Tile, Tub
and Grout Cleaner
16 oz., $7.95

Naturally Yours Basin,
Tub and Tile Cleaner
32 oz., $5

Mold and Mildew Removers

Enviro-Magic Mildew
Stain Away
16 oz., $9.95

Naturally Yours Mold
and Mildew Remover
32 oz., $5

Delimer

Naturally Yours
Delimer/Descaler
32 oz., $7

Around the House

Avoid conventional wood-furniture polishes, which can cause skin irritation; drain cleaners, which often contain dangerous chemicals (and are not always effective); and insect repellents, which contain a variety of toxic chemicals.

Air Fresheners
Earth Friendly
Uni-Fresh
4.4 oz., $4.99

Ecco Mist Air
Freshener
8 oz., $10.22

Naturally Yours
Natural Deodorizer
32 oz., $10

Carpet Cleaners
Bi-O-Kleen Fiber Glow
Liquid Concentrate
Carpet Cleaner
1 gallon, $24.74

Capture Dry Carpet
Cleaner
8 lbs., $34.95

Earth Friendly Rug
Shampoo
40 oz., $7.69

Naturally Yours
Carpet and
Upholstery Shampoo
32 oz., $7

Seventh Generation
Carpet Cleaner,
Natural Citrus
32 oz., $5.49

Drain Cleaners
Citra-Solv Citra-Drain
Natural Enzymatics
22 oz., $5.65

Earth Friendly Earth
Enzymes
2 lbs., $9.99

Naturally Yours
Enz-Away
32 oz., $7

Floor Soap
Ecover Natural Floor
Soap
32 oz., $4.09

Hope's Floor Revive
16 oz., $6.99

Natural Choices Clean
& Free Floor Cleaner
Concentrate
8 oz., $7.95

Fruit and Vegetable Wash

Bi-O-Kleen Produce
Wash
16 oz., $4.89

Earth Friendly Fruit
and Veggie Wash
22 oz., $4.59

Vermont Soaps Fruit
and Veggie Wash
16 oz., $7.98

Furniture Polish

Caldrea Wood
Furniture Cream
8 oz., $10

Earth Friendly
Furniture Polish
22 oz., $5.99

Enviro-Magic Lemon
Oil Furniture Polish
8 oz., $7.95

Mrs. Meyer's Wood
Furniture Cream
8.75 oz., $7.99

Natural Choices
Natural Shine Wood
Cleaner and Polish
8 oz., $6.95

Naturally Yours
Furniture Cleaner/
Protector Oil
32 oz., $7

Paper Products

Earth Friendly Orange
Plus Cleaning Towels,
Abrasive
70 towels, $7.49

Earth Friendly Orange
Plus Cleaning Towels,
Non-Abrasive
70 Towels, $5.59

Earth Friendly Paper
Towels
roll, $1.98

Method All-Purpose
Wipes
30 Wipes, $4

Seventh Generation
Paper Towels
roll, $2

Pest Control

Kness Pro Ketch
Mousetrap
$12.99

Kness Ants-No-More
Ant Bait Gel Formula
2 tubes, $22

Orange Guard Pest
Control
32 oz. bottle, $9

Victor Tin Cat
Repeating Mouse Trap
$11.99

Pet Care

Doc Ackerman's
Botanical Citronella
Pet Spray
20 oz., $9.99

Earth Friendly
Natumate Pet Stain
and Odor Remover
22 oz., $5.59

Feline Pine Cat Litter
20 lbs., $11.99

HomeoPet Flea Bite
15 ml, $13

Vermont Soaps
Organic Pet Shampoo
16 oz., $9.99

World's Best Cat Litter
17 lbs., $13.49

Stainless Steel Cleaners

Caldrea Stainless
Steel Spray
11.8 oz., $10

Hope's Stainless
Steel Polish
8 oz., $5.95

Method Stainless
Steel Cleaner
12 oz., $5

Mrs. Meyer's Stainless
Steel Scrub
15.7 oz., $7.99

Where to Buy

Nationwide

Bed, Bath & Beyond
www.bedbathandbeyond.com
The Container Store
www.containerstore.com
The Great Indoors
www.thegreatindoors.com
Home Depot
www.homedepot.com
Real Goods
gaiam.com/realgoods.com
Sur La Table
www.surlatable.com
Target
www.target.com
Trader Joe's
www.traderjoes.com
Whole Foods
www.wholefoods.com
Wild Oats
www.wildoats.com

West Coast

Henry's Market Place
www.wildoats.com
(CA)
Larry's Markets
www.larrysmarkets.com
(WA)
Mollie Stone's Markets
(CA)
www.molliestones.com
New Seasons Market
www.newseasonsmarket.com
(OR)
Zupan's Market
www.zupans.com
(OR)

Midwest

Akin's Natural Foods Market
www.akins.com
(OK, MO, NE, KS)
Jungle Jims
www.junglejims.com
(OH)
Merchant of Vino
www.wholefoods.com
(MI)

South

Central Market
www.centralmarket.com
(TX)
EarthFare
www.earthfare.com
(NC, SC, TN, GA)
Fresh Market
www.freshmarket.com
(AL, FL, GA, KY, SC, TN, VA)
Harry's Farmers Market
www.wholefoods.com
(GA)
Wellspring Grocery
www.wholefoods.com
(NC)

East Coast

Balducci's
www.balduccis.com
(CT, DC, MD, NY, VA)
Bowl & Board
www.bowlandboard.com
(MA)
Fresh Fields Markets
www.wholefoods.com
(NJ, VA, DC, MD, PA)
Mrs. Green's Natural Market
www.mrsgreens.com
(CT, NY)

Online

Drugstore.com
www.drugstore.com
Gaiam
www.gaiam.com
Green Home
www.greenhome.com
Green Living Now
www.greenlivingnow.com
Green People
www.greenpeople.org
Kokopelli's Green Market
www.kokogm.com
Lifekind Products
www.lifekind.com
Only Natural Pet Store
www.onlynaturalpet.com
Peaceful Company
www.apeacefulco.com
Real Goods
www.realgoods.com

Company Contact Information

A

Arm and Hammer
www.armandhammer.com
(800) 524-1328

B

Bi-O-Kleen
www.bi-o-kleen.com
(360) 576-0064
(800) 477-0188

Bio Pac
www.bio-pac.com
(866) 369-1385

Bon Ami
www.faultless.com

C

Cal Ben Soap Company
www.calbenpuresoap.com
(510) 638-7091
(800) 340-7091

The Caldrea Company
www.caldrea.com
(877) 576-8808

Capture Dry Carpet
Cleaner
www.captureclean.com
(800) 227-8873

Citra-Solv
www.citra-solv.com
(203) 778-0881

D

Dial 20 Mule Team Borax
www.dialcorp.com
(800) 528-0849

Doc Ackerman's Pet
Products
www.docackerman.com

Dr. Bronner Magic Soaps
www.drbronners.com
(760) 743-2211

E

Earth Friendly Products
www.ecos.com
(800) 335-3267

Ecover
www.ecover.com

Enviro-Magic
www.amazonpp.com
(305) 757-1943
(800) 832-5645

F

Feline Pine
www.naturesearth.com
(800) 749-7463

H

Heinz
www.heinz.com
(800) 255-5750

HomeoPet
www.homeopet.com
(800) 555-4461

The Hope Company
www.hopecompany.com
(314) 739-7254

K

Kirk's Natural Products
www.kirksnatural.com
(708) 771-5475
(800) 825-4757

Kness
www.kness.com
(641) 932-7846
(800) 247-5062

L

Lifekind
www.lifekind.com
(800) 284-4983

M

Method
www.methodhome.com
(866) 963-8463

Mrs. Meyer's Clean Day
www.mrsmeyers.com
(877) 865-1508

N

Natural Choices
www.oxyboost.com
(414) 421-9394
(866) 699-2667

Naturally Yours
www.naturallyyoursclean.com
(417) 889-3995

O

Orange Guard
www.orangeguard.com
(888) 659-3217

S

Seventh Generation
www.seventhgen.com
(802) 658-3773
(800) 456-1191

Shaklee
www.shaklee.com
(925) 924-2000
(800) 742-5533

Sun and Earth
www.sunandearth.com
(800) 298-7861

V

Vermont Soapworks
www.vermontsoap.com
(802) 388-4302
(866) 762-7482

Victor Pest
www.victorpest.com
(800) 800-1819

W

World's Best Cat Litter
www.worldsbestcatlitter.com
(877) 367-9225

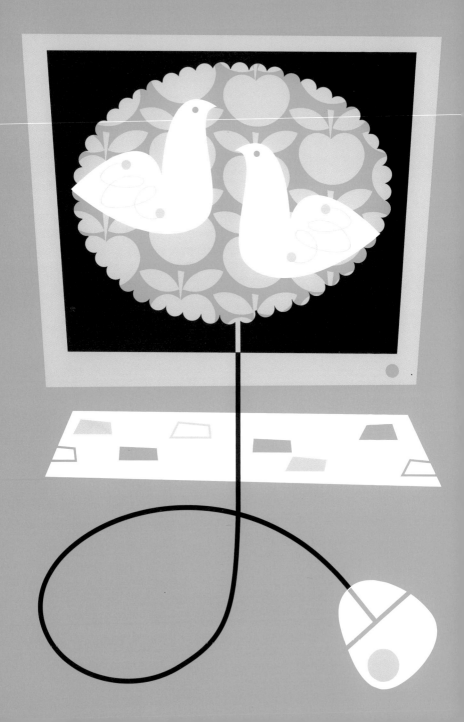

Chapter
11 : RESOURCES & READINGS

Bookstores, magazine racks, and the Internet are flush with information on chemicals, cleaners, and green living. The best resources for learning more about toxics include the EPA's exhaustive website and Seventh Generation's excellent *Guide to a Toxin-Free Home*. For broader tips on healthier, greener lifestyles, start with the *Green Guide* or one of the many whole-living-oriented magazines.

The American Lung Association Health House

The American Lung Association Health House resources include tip sheets that help you identify and reduce pollutants in your home and a list of builders who comply with the ALA's Healthy House Builders Guidelines.
www.healthhouse.org

The Center for the New American Dream

The Center for the New American Dream works with businesses, communities, and individuals to conserve natural resources and change the way goods are produced and consumed. "The Conscious Consumer" section of its website recommends environmentally friendly choices for everything from coffee to lightbulbs.
www.newdream.org

Co-Op America

Co-Op America is a nonprofit organization that provides strategies and practical tools for businesses and individuals to address environmental and social problems such as petroleum depletion and sweatshop labor. They publish informa-tion about conscientious investing as well as the Green Pages (see page 176).
www.coopamerica.org

Energy Star

The Energy Star symbol appears on appliances that meet strict requirements determined by the EPA and U.S. Department of Energy. The Energy Star website offers information on how to make your current home more energy efficient, as well as what to look for when building a new home.
www.energystar.gov

The Environmental Protection Agency

The EPA provides extensive information on everything from household hazardous waste to environmental technology, as well as links to educational resources and electronic versions of the country's environmental laws and regulations.
www.epa.gov

GreenClips

Architectural researcher and environmental consultant Chris Hammer publishes *GreenClips,* a summary of news about sustainable building design and related government and business issues. The newsletter is posted on the website and e-mailed to members every two weeks.
www.greenclips.com

Green Guide

The Green Guide, published six times a year, provides information on everything from green cleaning products to nontoxic toys. With an extensive, easy-to-use product guide, helpful message boards,

and coupons for green products, it is an indispensable resource for those trying to lead a greener life.
www.thegreenguide.com

Green Home Building
The Green Home Building website provides a wide range of information on sustainable architecture.
www.greenhomebuilding.com

Green Pages
The Green Pages is the largest online directory of qualified green business, listing more than 25,000 products and services from 2,000 companies.
www.coopamerica.org/pubs/greenpages

Green Seal
The Green Seal organization is dedicated to achieving a healthier and cleaner environment by identifying and promoting products and services that create less toxic pollution and waste and that conserve resources. Their website includes detailed product recommendations in their "Choose Green Reports."
www.greenseal.org

InForm
InForm is a nonprofit organization that examines the effects of business practices on human health and the environment. One of their main focuses is toxic chemicals and human health. InForm's Purchasing for Pollution Prevention Project helps federal, state, and local governments purchase safer alternatives to certain toxic cleaning products.
www.informinc.org

Lifekind Chemical Glossary
Lifekind, which sells a wide range of green household products, publishes a helpful and comprehensive guide to household chemicals on its website.
www.lifekind.com/catalog/chemical_glossary.php

National Institutes of Health Household Products Database
The National Institutes of Health's National Library of Medicine provides detailed information on a variety of commercial cleaning products. Information includes health effects, emergency first-aid procedures, chemical content, and disposal information.
www.householdproducts.nlm.nih.gov/

Natural Resources Defense Council
The Natural Resources Defense Council is an independent organization that strives to protect the environment through activism, law, and science. NRDC's website provides a wealth of environmental information, including resources on toxic chemicals and indoor air pollution. The website also includes state-of-the-art online activism tools.
www.nrdc.org

Washington Toxic Coalition
The Washington Toxic Coalition works to protect public health by eliminating toxic pollution. Their website includes detailed information on ridding the home of toxic chemicals and protecting your children from toxic exposure.
www.watoxics.org

Books

An Inconvenient Truth by Al Gore (Rodale, 2006)
An investigation of the climate crisis by the former Vice President detailing the harm humans are causing the planet, and what we can do to fix it.

Baking Soda by Vicki Lansky (Book Peddlers, 2004)
More than 500 uses for baking soda, from making cookies to bee sting relief and cutting grease in your pots and pans.

Better Basics for the Home by Annie Berthold-Bond (Three Rivers Press, 1999)
Practical tips for building a simpler, healthier lifestyle from a leading authority on environmentally safe practices.

Cradle to Cradle by William McDonough and Michael Braungart (North Point Press, 2002)
A visionary treatise on the future of industry, when products and their materials are designed for long lives, rather than for the landfill.

Creating a Safe and Healthy Home by Linda Mason Hunter (Creative Publishing International, 2005)
A comprehensive guide to keeping your home healthy, covering topics from indoor air quality to hazardous waste storage to selecting the right furniture.

Field Guide to Stains by Virginia M. Friedman, Melissa Wagner, and Nancy Armstrong (Quirk Books, 2002)
Step-by-step tips on identifying and removing a plethora of stains.

Home Comforts: The Art & Science of Keeping House by Cheryl Mendelson (Scribner, 1999)
The be-all and end-all reference on contemporary home economics. Mendelson's thoroughness is unparalleled.

Home Safe Home, Protecting Yourself and Your Family from Everyday Toxics and Harmful Household Products in the Home by Debra Lynn Dadd (Tarcher, 1997)
Some 400 tips, do-it-yourself formulas, and pieces of advice on how to create a toxic-free home.

How to Grow Fresh Air: 50 Houseplants That Purify Your Home or Office by B.C. Wolverton (Penguin, 1997)
The culmination of more than 25 years of research, *How to Grow Fresh Air* stresses the importance of indoor air quality and how houseplants can play an integral role in improving quality of life.

Let it Rot! The Gardener's Guide to Composting by Stu Campbell (Storey Publishing, 1998)
A comprehensive guide to composting, complete with how-to diagrams and a reference guide.

The Naturally Clean Home by Karyn Siegel-Maier (Storey Publishing, 1999)
Includes more than 100 natural recipes for alternatives to traditional, toxic cleaning supplies.

Magazines

The Safe Shopper's Bible, A Consumer's Guide to Nontoxic Household Products, Cosmetics and Food by David Steinman and Samuel S. Epstein, M.D. (Macmillan, 1995)
Identifies the most dangerous cleaning products, cosmetics, and food on the market and recommends healthy and safe alternatives.

The Seventh Generation Guide to a Toxin-Free Home
available online from Seventh Generation at *www.seventhgen.com/living_green/ toxin_free.php*
With in-depth research and statistics, the *Seventh Generation Guide to a Toxin-Free Home* makes a compelling argument for using safer alternatives to traditional cleaning products.

Vinegar by Vicki Lansky (Book Peddlers, 2004)
This sequel to *Baking Soda* explores hundreds of household uses for vinegar.

WorldChanging: A User's Guide for the 21st Century edited by Alex Steffen (Abrams, 2006)
An encyclopedia of how to change the world both locally and globally, covering topics from living off the grid to making socially responsible investments.

Body and Soul
www.bodyandsoulmag.com

E/The Environmental Magazine
www.emagazine.com

Home Energy Magazine
www.homeenergy.org

Natural Health
www.naturalhealthmag.com

Natural Home
www.naturalhomemagazine.com

Plenty
www.plentymag.com

Real Simple
www.realsimple.com

Utne Reader
www.utne.com

Yoga Journal's Balanced Living
www.yogajournal.com

Recycling & Disposal

The best source of recycling and disposal information for your community is your local department of sanitation or waste management; some cities rely on private carting services. Many municipalities have extensive recycling and disposal resources online; start with your city or county's website.

Earth 911
The Earth 911 website has detailed information on recycling everything from aluminum cans to old computers and provides extensive local resources.
www.earth911.org

Environmental Hazards Management Institute
EHMI publishes the Household Product Management Wheel, which offers practical information and tips on managing 36 commonly used household chemical products — from purchase to disposal/recycling. They also offer an auto recycling wheel, a home inventory wheel, and a composting wheel; they are $10 each.
10 Newmarket Road
Durham, NH 03821
(800) 558-3464
www.ehspublishing.com/products

EPA Resources on Household Hazardous Waste
The EPA provides information on household hazardous waste management, disposal, and reduction. The website includes a list of common household products that contain potentially hazardous materials, as well as alternatives to these products, and disposal and collection details.
www.epa.gov/epaoswer/non-hw/househld/hhw.htm

Municipal Solid Waste Collection by State
This website provides links to the Division of Solid and Hazardous Materials for each state. The state websites provide information on recycling, household hazardous waste management and disposal, and state assistance programs.
www.epa.gov/garbage/states.htm

University of Missouri's Household Hazardous Waste Project
A great resource that provides information on how to dispose of common household products, including automotive and cleaning products. Disposing of paint and pesticides is addressed in detail.
outreach.missouri.edu/owm/hhw.htm

Carpet Reclamation

Interface
*www.interfaceinc.com/us/services/
Reclamation/*

Milliken Carpet Earth Square
www.earthsquare.com

Cell Phones

Call2Recycle
(also takes rechargeable batteries)
www.rbrc.org/call2recycle

Motorola
www.racetorecycle.com

Cingular
www.cingular.com/about/recycling

Sprint
*www.sprint.com/community/
communities_across/spc.html*

T-Mobile
www.t-mobile.com/company/recycling/

Verizon
*aboutus.vzw.com/communityservice/
hopeLineRecycling.html*

Computers

Apple
www.apple.com/environment/recycling

Dell
www.dell.com/recycling

Greendisk
www.greendisk.com

National Cristina Program
www.cristina.org

Foam Packaging

EPS Packaging
www.epspackaging.org/info.html

Freecycling & Reuse
Freecycle

The idea that one person's trash is another person's treasure is put into action at Freecycle.org. The website is an electronic forum for individuals and non-profits to "recycle" unwanted goods. You can find anything from a fax machine to a piano on this website.
www.freecycle.org

Grass Roots Recycling Network

The Grass Roots Recycling Network is a nonprofit organization dedicated to eliminating the waste of human and natural resources. Their Zero Waste program is a design program for the 21st century that encourages businesses to be responsible for their products from "cradle to cradle."
www.grrn.org

Reuse Development Organization

A state-by-state guide to local reuse centers for everything from building materials to furniture.
www.redo.org/FindReuse.html

Composting
Compost Guide

This is a basic but useful online manual to composting It includes charts on common composting materials, as well as information on troubleshooting composting problems.
www.compostguide.com

How to Compost

The How to Compost website is a hub for all things composting. For beginners or the experienced composter, the website is a great resource.
www.howtocompost.org

Index

This Book Is Not a Tree

A Note about *Green Clean*

Green Clean is a DuraBook, a waterproof, stain-resistant, super-durable book made with synthetic paper and a special binding. It will last for years — carted around the house, sitting out in the sun, soaked in a cleaning bucket.

You might expect that a guide to ecofriendly housecleaning would be made of recycled paper. But recycling can only be done so many times; fibers eventually lose their strength and the paper becomes garbage.

The materials we use do not need to become trash. Instead, they can become nutrients for a new generation of goods. "Waste equals food," architect William McDonough and chemist Michael Braungart write in their landmark book *Cradle to Cradle.* They describe the coming transformation of industry from one "that takes, makes, and wastes to one that celebrates natural, economic, and cultural abundance."

Green Clean represents a step toward this more sustainable way of making things. The polypropylene that *Green Clean* is printed on, which can be traditionally recycled, will, in a better industrial system, become just such a nutrient, part of a stream of materials that can be reused over and over without losing their integrity.

As *Green Clean*'s authors note, a tool that lasts for years is an ecofriendly tool. If you are done with *Green Clean,* though, a landfill is no place for a book. Give it to a friend or a library, or send it to us at Melcher Media. We will make sure it is properly recycled.

For more information on green cleaning and DuraBooks, visit *www.greencleanbook.com.*

MELCHER
MEDIA
124 W. 13th Street
New York, NY 10011
www.melcher.com